Avril le Roux

the JAR SPELLS

Compendium

~

Unleash Your Magic And Enhance Your Craft With 100 Witch Bottles Recipes For Protection, Abundance, Love, Healing and More

© Copyright 2022 by Avril Le Roux - All rights reserved.

All rights reserved. No part of this book may be reproduced in any form without permission in writing from the author. Reviewers may quote brief passages in reviews.

While all attempts have been made to verify the information provided in this publication, neither the author nor the publisher assumes any responsibility for errors, omissions, or contrary interpretation of the subject matter herein.

The views expressed in this publication are those of the author alone and should not be taken as expert instruction or commands. The reader is responsible for his or her own actions, as well as his or her own interpretation of the material found within this publication.

Adherence to all applicable laws and regulations, including international, federal, state and local governing professional licensing, business practices, advertising, and all other aspects of doing business in the US, Canada or any other jurisdiction is the sole responsibility of the reader and consumer.

Neither the author nor the publisher assumes any responsibility or liability whatsoever on behalf of the consumer or reader of this material. Any perceived slight of any individual or organization is purely unintentional.

TABLE OF CONTENTS

Introduction 7
What You Will Find in This Book 7
- Chapter 1 - Witchcraft yesterday and today 9
    - A Hint Of The Past 10
    - Witchcraft Today 12
    - Differences Between Witchcraft, Paganism And Wicca 13
    - Conclusions 15
- Chapter 2 - Spell Jars 16
    - History of the Magic Potions 17
    - Magic Potions Today 17
    - Where to Start? 18
    - The container 18
- Chapter 3 - First Steps In Witchcraft 20
    - What is a Witch? 21
    - Are Witches Born or Become? 22
    - Preparing for a Ritual 23
- Chapter 4 - Jar Spell Recipes for Protection 25
    - Witch Bottle For Personal Protection 26
    - Witch Bottle For House Protection 27
    - Witch's Bottle For The Protection Of Spaces 28
    - Witch's Bottle For The Protection Of One's Animals 29
    - Witch Bottle For The Protection Of Children And Infants 30
    - Witch's Bottle For Negative Vibes 31
    - Bottle Of The Witch For The Protection Of The Family 32
    - Witch's Bottle To Protect The House From Spirits 33
    - Witch's Bottle For Protection From The Envy Of Others 34
    - Witch's Bottle To Protect Oneself From Misfortune 35
    - Witch's Bottle To Protect Against Negative Influences 36
    - Witch Bottle For Protection From Thieves 37
    - Witch's Bottle To Protect Oneself From Assailants 38
    - Witch's Bottle of Generic Protection 39

Witch's Bottle To Protect One's Memories *40*
Witch Bottle To Protect Against Accidents *41*
Witch's Bottle To Protect Oneself From The Evil Eye *42*
Witch Bottle To Protect Beauty *43*
Witch Bottle To Protect Plants *44*
Witch Bottle To Protect Oneself From Addiction *45*

Chapter 5 - Jar Spell Recipes To Attract Love *46*

Witch Bottle To Attract Passionate Love *47*
Bottle Of The Witch To Attract Eternal Love *48*
Witch Bottle To Attract A Particular Person *49*
Witch Bottle To Bring An Ex Back *50*
Witch's Bottle to Strengthen an Extinguished Love. *51*
Witch Bottle To Seduce Someone *52*
Witch Bottle To Attract Eternal Love *53*
Witch Bottle To Increase Fertility *54*
Witch's Bottle To Avert Betrayal *55*
Witch's Bottle For Loving Yourself *56*
Witch Bottle to Foster Couple Communication. *57*
Witch Bottle For Magnetic Appeal *58*
Witch Bottle to Promote Coexistence *59*
Witch Bottle To Promote Marriage *60*
Witch Bottle to Make You Say "I Love You" *61*
Witch Bottle To Strengthen Your Feelings *62*
Witch Bottle for Clarity in the Sentimental Field *63*
Witch's Bottle For A United Family *64*
Witch Bottle To Mitigate Jealousy *65*
Witch Bottle To Rekindle Passion *66*

Chapter 6 - Jar Spell Recipes To Attract Wealth *67*

Introduction To Bottles For Attracting Wealth And Financial Prosperity *67*
Witch Bottle To Attract Small Amounts Of Money *68*
Witch Bottle To Safeguard One's Wealth *69*
Witch Bottle To Attract Large Sums Of Money *70*
Witch Bottle To Attract Prosperity *71*
Witch Bottle To Attract Financial Well-Being *72*

Witch Bottle to Attract a Promotion at Work 73
Witch Bottle To Make a Business Flourish Again. 74
Witch Bottle for a Successful Idea. 75
Witch's Bottle To Make The Right Decision 76
Witch Bottle For Being Influential 77
Witch Bottle To Banish Procrastination 78
Bottle Of The Millionaire's Witch 79
Witch Bottle To Ward Off Debt 80
Witch Bottle To Get A Mortgage Or Loan 81
Witch's Bottle For Living In Abundance 82
Witch Bottle For The Event 83
Witch Bottle for the Full Wallet. 84
Witch's Bottle To Recover A Lost Sum 85
Witch Bottle to Counter Wastefulness 86
Witch Bottle To Counteract Avarice 87

Chapter 7 - Jar Spell Recipes To Attract Good Luck 88

Witch Bottle To Attract Luck In Love 89
Witch Bottle To Get Your Dream Job 90
Witch Bottle To Attract Luck In The Lottery 91
Witch Bottle To Attract Luck In Sports 92
Witch's Bottle To Find A Lost Object 93
Witch Bottle To Banish Bad Luck 94
Witch Bottle To Be In The Right Place At The Right Time 95
Witch Bottle To Stay Healthy All The Time 96
Witch Bottle To Make A Wish Come True 97
Witch Bottle To Attract Luck In A Specific Area 98
Witch's Bottle For The Sex Of The Unborn Child 99
Witch Bottle for Renewal of Labor Contract. 100
Witch Bottle To Receive The Perfect Gift 101
Witch Bottle To Find The Car Of Your Dreams 102
Bottle of the Witch to Find Your Dream Home. 103
Witch's Bottle To Always Have Good Luck 104
Witch's Bottle for a Lucky Meeting 105
To Always Arrive On Time. 106

Witch Bottle To Always Find Parking 107
Witch Bottle To Bestow Good Fortune On Someone 108

Chapter 8- Jar Spell Recipes For Physical And Spiritual Healing 109

Witch Bottle To Propitiate Calmness 110
Witch Bottle To Ward Off Nightmares 111
Witch Bottle To Propitiate Creativity 112
Witch Bottle For Emotional Healing 113
Witch's Bottle To Propitiate Forgiveness And Let It Flow 114
Witch Bottle For Healing From Childhood Trauma 115
Witch's Bottle For Inner Peace 116
Witch Bottle To Promote Acceptance 117
Witch's Bottle For Lucid Dreams 118
Witch's Bottle For Astral Travel 119
Witch's Bottle To Replenish Energy 120
Witch Bottle To Purify From Negative Energies 121
Bottle of Witch for Gratitude 122
Witch's Bottle For Happiness 123
Witch's Bottle To Overcome a Disappointment 124
Witch Bottle for Family Serenity 125
Witch Bottle To Boost Self-Confidence 126
Witch's Bottle To Reach A Healthy Weight 127
Witch Bottle To Stop Thinking Too Much 128
Witch Bottle For The Here And Now 129

Conclusion 130

INTRODUCTION

Magic, and all it encompasses, has been a source of inspiration, curiosity and awe for human beings since ancient times. The search for answers related to the meaning of life, the creation of the universe and what makes it up, and why certain things happen have assumed a dominant role in human life since they learned to communicate.

Human beings are distinguished from every other living race by the visceral need to get an answer to everything that does not have one. Magic is one of those subjects around which thousands of conflicting opinions exist. Yet, as is the case with every intangible thing, which we cannot perceive through the use of the five senses, we can never get certain and unambiguous answers.

This is also why Magic possesses an enduring appeal. Humans, desperate to attribute logical and measurable meaning to anything, are consequently attracted to anything they cannot measure and categorize. In the worst cases, as history teaches, they can condemn what they do not understand or is beyond their control.

What You Will Find in This Book

Welcome to your compendium of Witchcraft Bottles. If you have this book in your hands—whether you bought it or given to you by someone—it means that you have taken seriously the idea of starting to practice Witchcraft. But whether this is your first book on the subject, or you are a Witch with some basic knowledge already, if you are looking for an in-depth look at magical potions and rituals, this is the right guide for you.

This book will guide you through discovering what potions are, how to use them to your advantage to attract protection, love, happiness, abundance, health and more to you, and how to harness the power of Witch Bottles to give you and your loved ones a prosperous future.

No special skills or prior experience are required to succeed in creating your first Witch Bottle. Within this compendium, you will find easy-to-make recipes that will allow you to create your first potions right away, with ingredients that

are easy to find. For ingredients that are more complicated to find, such as moon eclipse water, substitutes will be suggested in each recipe, so that even novice Witches who do not have a large larder of ingredients can try their hand at creating potions serenely.

At the end of this book, you will also find a handbook that will enable you to acquire the proper knowledge to create your personalized Witch Bottles all by yourself through deep knowledge of ingredients, colors, moon phases and more. But before that happens, we will tackle the journey of creating Witch Bottles together through the tried-and-true recipes in this compendium so that you can enjoy the creation process without fear.

While reading this book, all your questions about magic potions, the tools you need, and the benefits you will derive from them will be answered practically and concisely. I know that the expectation is very high, and you can't wait to get started, but for now put your doubts and worries aside and let these pages carry you through, with the knowledge that everything you need to take your first steps into the world of Witchcraft and become a Witch is contained in this book.

Happy reading,

Avril Le Roux

-CHAPTER 1-

WITCHCRAFT YESTERDAY AND TODAY

Witchcraft is a practice as old as human beings themselves. Humans have always sought answers to what they could not understand, such as the cycle of life, nature, weather, luck, and anything that seems, even on the surface, to fall outside "logic."

The history of Witchcraft is unfortunately indelibly marked by the deaths of the thousands persecuted and killed during the centuries of the Inquisition. Practicing witchcraft was equivalent to being devoted to the devil and acting through it. Today Witchcraft is no longer seen as a sinful practice, so much so that one can be a Witch and belong to a Cult or Religion. In this chapter, we will look at the history of Witchcraft over the centuries, what it meant to be Witches 600 years ago and what it means to be Witches today. We will then address the much-discussed topic of the differences between Witchcraft, paganism, and Wicca.

A Hint Of The Past

December 5, 1484, was the day Pope Innocent VII opened the Witch Hunt, kicking off a bloody and tremendous persecution of enormous proportions that claimed an untold number of victims, an estimated fifty thousand in Europe alone.

Founded in the 12th century, the Inquisition was considered, if one can call it that, the police organ of the Church and was tasked with investigating the proponents of theories considered contrary to Catholic orthodoxy—the so-called "heresies." It was only with Pope John XXII and his bull *Super illius specula* (1326) that the jurisdiction of the inquisitors was extended to persons suspected of engaging in acts of Witchcraft, which from then on was considered a heretical practice.

In 1487, three years after the start of the Witch Hunt, the *Malleus Maleficarum* ("The Hammer of Witches") was published, a treatise written by Heinrich Kramer and Jacob Sprenger, the two Dominican friars to whom the pope granted full inquisitorial powers to counter and suppress Witchcraft in Germany. In this treatise, a veritable witch-hunting manual, Kramer and Sprenger gave free rein to all their wickedness. Within it were strategies on how to effectively recognize a witch, how to capture her, how to extract a confession from her through disparate torture techniques, and finally how to try her and condemn her to the stake.

The Malleus Maleficarum quickly gained fame throughout Europe until it became the undisputed and most effective tool for recognizing any link between woman and devil. All 16th-century inquisitors were instructed and trained based

on this treatise.

The Witchcraft persecution affected Europe, especially France, Germany, Italy, Switzerland, Luxembourg, the Netherlands and today's Belgium. Still, the advent of the printing press ensured that the phenomenon spread overseas, eventually reaching America, creating a true collective psychosis.

Although there is no certain number of casualties caused by the Witch Hunt, as the Church has lost or concealed part of the records concerning the 13th century Inquisition, we know that the persecution had an enormous scope: we speak of thousands and thousands of victims.

Most of the people accused of Witchcraft and having links with the devil were women (over 70 percent), especially widows without someone who could defend them. Even elderly women who used to prepare herbal remedies were in the crosshairs of the Inquisition.

But why women in particular?

Beyond the fact that they were weaker and more helpless than the male sex, the truth lies in that physicians of the time knew very little about female being, and theologians labeled them as inconstant and indocile individuals who needed to be tamed by a male figure. Formerly the property of their father, once married they became their husband's property. It was only as widows, therefore, that they could achieve a certain autonomy and, in the absence of someone to supervise them, according to the beliefs of the time, be able to then "deviate" into heretical practices.

In a society where a woman's social position was well regarded only within a family unit as a wife and mother, the women most at risk were those who had relative autonomy, and thus the opportunity to increase their knowledge, such as those who knew how to use medicinal herbs to heal (medichesse) or experienced midwives who could terminate unwanted pregnancies.

When a woman considered a witch or associated with Witchcraft was identified, she was subjected to the practice described in Malleus Maleficarum. It began with the search for the Devil's Mark, that is, the tangible sign of the witch's pact with the Devil, which could be a mole or a spot on the skin that was "insensitive to pain." The woman was shaved completely by appointees, who carefully studied every spot on her body, and then a needle was stuck on every mole, wart, birthmark or skin discoloration. If the passage of the needle did not cause pain and bleeding on one of them, the latter was considered a diabolical mark and proof of the actual bond between the woman and the devil. But in the Malleus Maleficarum, this was not the only torture to which to subject a suspect. One

could opt to throw the woman into the water, with bound hands and feet, in places considered "blessed." If the body sank, there was no trace of Witchcraft. On the contrary, if the body floated, then that was proof that one was dealing with a witch. Unfortunately, this practice also caused the accidental drowning of women considered innocent; in this regard, they opted to tie a rope to the women's torso so they could be brought back to the surface if they sank. However, the risk of drowning remained very high.

These are just a few examples, but the torture methods were countless.

Before the grueling interrogation to which the accused were subjected, they were weighed. Indeed, it was believed that Witches weighed less than the norm. In the Netherlands, for example, women were weighed on the Heksen Waag, the "Witches' scale," dressed only in a paper gown: if the weight was excessive according to what were the imposed rules, the charges fell since it was evident that the weight would not allow them to fly on a broom.

During interrogation, the defendants might be asked to recite the Bible from memory. The slightest error or hesitation in pronunciation was declared an unmistakable sign of Evil.

If the woman was found guilty, she was usually sentenced to burn at the stake, but not always. What is considered the last Witch executed was sentenced to be beheaded: she was a woman of humble origins named Anna Göldi, and she was killed in Switzerland in June 1782.

Witchcraft Today

The historical hint given to you above was not written to demoralize or frighten you, but to get an overview of what happened to those accused of practicing Sorcery. Back then no distinctions were made about the types of Witchcraft practiced, whether Green, White or Black. Any Witch, regardless of what goal she pursued, was condemned for having direct dealings with the devil. Fortunately, today Witchcraft can be practiced by anyone who wishes to have direct contact with the occult sphere, to improve their lives ethically by developing direct contact with the irrational part of the human being.

Practicing Witchcraft nowadays is no longer synonymous with having established a connection with the devil. One can practice Witchcraft with peace of mind while respecting one's religion, if one pursues one.

Deciding not to practice Black Magic is a choice dictated by each individual's conscience. However, being a Witch is not only a choice but very often a necessi-

ty, a path compelled by one's nature. Some feel they are a Witch at an early age; those who approach Witchcraft very early because it is a practice handed down from their family, and those who discover it later, becoming interested by chance. Some feel a special connection with the four elements; those who are more sensitive than others, those who have strong empathy, and those who believe they have no special gifts but feel different. Whoever you are, whoever you have been, it does not matter. What matters is that you believe in yourself and deeply understand who you are. The rest will come to you.

Differences Between Witchcraft, Paganism And Wicca

Very often, especially among neophytes, there is a tendency to use the appellation Wicca to address anything related to magic and Witchcraft. This term, however, is used incorrectly. Indeed, it is correct to say that a Wiccan is a Witch, but it is incorrect to say that a Witch is, as a result, a Wiccan. Likewise, it is correct to say that a Wiccan is a pagan, but not the other way around. Why?

Paganism is the set of pagan cults. The term "pagan" is derived from the Latin paganus and was used to refer to the inhabitant of the pagus, a type of country village, and therefore this term was used with the meaning of "villager" or "peasant." However, with the Edict of Thessalonica promulgated in 380 A.D. by the emperors Gratian, Valentinian II and Theodosius, Christianity became the only accepted religion in the Empire, and its spread in urban centers was very rapid. Conversely, in more remote areas-and thus in the pagus-the conversion was slow, which is why the peasants continued to practice polytheism. Then, the term "pagan" changed meaning and began to refer to all those who, contrary to the laws of the Empire, continued to practice polytheism.

Today modern paganism is known as neo-paganism, and it is the set of religions, traditions and spiritual movements that draw on ancient paganism. Among these religions, we find Wicca.

Wicca is in effect a religion, and at its basis we find the opposition of the two cosmic principles, the God and the Goddess, which together form the One. There is a strong belief in reincarnation in Wicca, and in general, it is characterized by a deep-rooted ethic, dogma and precise rules to be followed. In essence, the Wiccan is a pagan who has consciously adhered to the neopagan cult of Wicca. A pagan, on the other hand, has adhered to a cult and possesses his spirituality without necessarily being part of the Wiccan religion. Other neopagan cults are Druidism, based on Celtic religion, Odinism, which draws on the mythologi-

cal-religious traditions of the ancient Germans and Scandinavians, and shamanism. Among them they share common practices such as the celebration of Sabbats and the use of aids such as herbs and crystals.

A Wiccan, thus one who has consciously adhered to the cult of Wicca, believes of the One, which is the Source of Everything and is Infinite. The One is composed of the God and the Goddess, the two opposites that shape the energy that permeates everything together. The duality that makes up this cult relates to life itself: everything has its opposite. Life and death are opposites but are seen in the form of a circle, so it is not just death that follows life, but life that follows death, and hence the strong belief in reincarnation as a direct consequence of the cyclical nature of existence. Wicca is divided into several streams, including Gardnerian Wicca and Alexandrian Wicca.

Wicca and Witchcraft share many aspects, so neophytes often confuse these two terms and use them indiscriminately. Still, one of the key differences is that Wicca is a religion, a spiritual path, a set of beliefs aimed at creating a harmonious and balanced lifestyle. At the same time, Witchcraft is the set of practices and rituals. One can therefore practice Witchcraft without being a Wiccan or a pagan.

Witchcraft, which will be the mainstay of this book, is developed by keeping an open mind and far from adhering to a religion specifically. One who practices Witchcraft can be defined in all respects as a Witch (both male and female). However, according to Scott Douglas Cunningham, a celebrated figure in the pagan community and author of books on Wicca considered to be among the most influential and revolutionary ever, one who practices Witchcraft is to be called a Wiccan, and not a Witch.

Usually in Witchcraft, the Witch practices alone, as a free and independent individual, and feels no need to bind herself to one or more deities. On the other hand, Wiccans are also often part of Witchcraft communities called "Covens."

Another substantial difference between Wicca and Witchcraft is that the former adopts the Law of Three, which was first found in a book by Gerald Gardner, which states, "everything we do comes back to us three times for good and three times for evil." For this reason, Wiccans do not practice Black Magic, expecting the evil inflicted to be returned three times over. However, this aspect is not present in Witchcraft, so there is no limitation to the types of magic that can be practiced. The limits are those imposed by one's Conscience and common sense.

Conclusions

As explained in the chapter just concluded, this handbook broadly covers Witchcraft's mysterious and fascinating world, without spiritual or religious limitations. It will be up to you to adapt what is contained in this compendium to your personal beliefs.

In the next chapter, we will address the specific topic of magic potions, what they are and how you can use them to improve your life and the lives of the people you love.

- Chapter 2 -

Spell Jars

In this chapter, we will look specifically at what Witch Bottles, also called "spell jars," are. They are nothing more than small bottles (or jars) with certain characteristics, inside which ingredients are placed to create a potion with a certain purpose, such as protecting, healing, attracting love and luck, and more.

But as much as Witch Bottle is a more current practice than ever, it actually has ancient origins. Let's take a dip into the past together.

History of the Magic Potions

The use of Witch Bottles dates back to the 17th century, as evidenced by numerous finds, including one in Greenwich, England, in 2009. Although these incredible discoveries are mostly associated with the United Kingdom, there has also been a famous find in Pennsylvania—the only one in all of America. Some archaeologists claim that only about a hundred Witch Bottles have survived intact to the present day, a number so small that it seems incredible that any have already been found to date.

Initially, Witch Bottles were considered a defensive tool: the bottle owners used them for protection against something specific. At that time, it was good practice to keep Witch Bottles at one's home to protect them, and it was not unusual to even wall them into the house walls.

Early Witch Bottles were made of ceramic or burnished glass, and inside them it was usual to find pins, bent and rusty nails, nails, hair, pubic hair, and sometimes even animal or human blood and urine.

Bottles of this kind were used until the 19th century, after which the use of such ingredients faded, although there may still be some hint of them. Alan Massey of Loughborough University states, "Items found in Witch Bottles verify the authenticity of contemporary recipes [...] that might otherwise have been deemed too outrageous or ridiculous to believe."

Magic Potions Today

In modern practices, the Witch Bottle is made of glass and filled with different ingredients for various purposes. Thus, not only to protect oneself from something but also to attract love, abundance, serenity, spiritual and physical health to oneself and others, and much more.

The Witch Bottle can be kept at home, or buried in one's garden or other personal property. If placed at the entrance to one's home, for example, it can act as a "sponge" for negative energies and trap them inside. Burying it in the farthest corner of one's property, on the other hand, helps keep away bad influences, the evil eye and evil-doers.

Where to Start?

Making a Witch Bottle does not require a lot of equipment. Everything you need to make one is readily available, or you may already own it in your home.

So let's see what tools are needed.

The container

While speaking of Witch Bottle, the first thing that comes to mind is, of course, a bottle. In reality, any container with a lid can serve the purpose very well. Ideally, it would be preferable to choose a non-transparent material, so yes to glass, but only if it is tinted or amber.

It is thought that the use of ceramics in earlier centuries was precisely due to the need to overcome the lack of non-transparent glass.

It is vitally important that the container you choose possesses a lid made of natural and not synthetic material, as with any other utensil used in Witchcraft, so plastic is banned. Yes to glass, ceramic and even cork.

- **Candles wax to seal the lid**

For the Witch Bottle to be complete, the lid (or cap) must be sealed with a candle wax. Candle colors have specific meanings that will be explained later, but generally, a red or a black candle will do.

- **Ingredients**

Of course, composing your Witch Bottle will require ingredients, which you can get depending on the type of spell you need. Don't worry, there will be no toadstools or dragon scales among the proposed ingredients. The potions in this book were created to be easy to make and composed of ingredients that are affordable and easy to obtain.

Some of the ingredients mentioned most often include nails, pins, rock salt, pennies, and herbs. Nothing eccentric or unobtainable.

- **The intention**

This is the last item on the list, but it is not in importance. You need to understand right now that intention is one of the indispensable elements of creating potions and spells. In Witchcraft, no rules prohibit you from doing one or the other, so the only limitation you have to rely on is common sense and your conscience. Before you do any potion or spell, you need to be clear about the intention behind that practice. Your intention should be:

  ◊ **Specific.**

You must be focused specifically on the result you want to achieve and concentrate solely and only on that. To be effective at its maximum expression, a spell cannot be done for several things at once, nor can it be done just for the sake of doing (thus in the absence of a real desire or need) or in too general a manner.

  ◊ **Achievable.**

What you want to achieve must not only be clear and defined, but also, and more importantly, realistic and achievable. The idea of creating spells and potions can make the imagination soar, but beware: stay grounded. Forget Professor Snape's potions in Harry Potter, that's fantasy.

  ◊ **Ethics.**

As I mentioned a few lines above, in Witchcraft there is nothing and no one that prohibits you from doing anything. Unlike Wicca, which follows the Law of Three, Witchcraft has no belief about the repercussions for those who use and practice Black Magic. Only you can decide how far to go and where to delineate the boundaries of your ethics, at your peril.

In this introductory chapter, we saw what magic potions are, their history over the centuries, and how they were prepared as early as the 17th century with ingredients that today we might call "macabre," such as urine, blood, and bodily fluids of various kinds. We then saw how this practice has evolved through the centuries, what has remained unchanged and what is considered "ethical" today. Finally, we learned how to start trying your hand at creating magical potions, what tools are needed to create potions, and the power of intention with its three basic pillars: specificity, achievability, and ethics. In the next chapter, we will delve into the basics of Witchcraft and see what it means to be a Witch today.

- CHAPTER 3 -

First Steps in Witchcraft

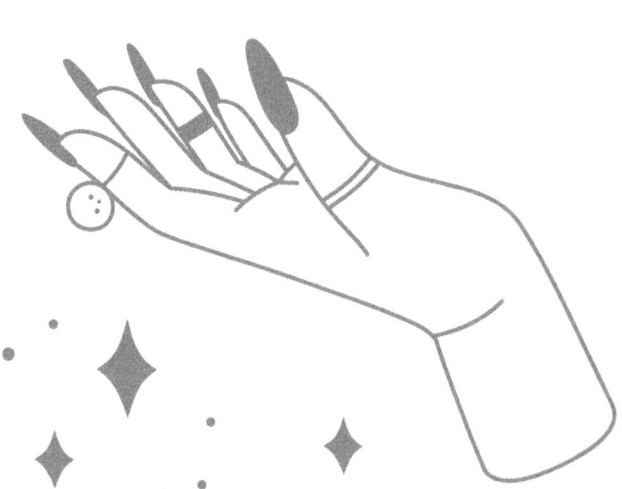

*I*n the previous chapter, we discovered what magic potions are and how to use them to our advantage. In this one, however, we will discuss what a Witch is, the debate that has always inflamed the world of Witchcraft: Are Witches Born or Become? Finally, we will discuss what actions are a good idea to follow to properly prepare for a ritual, purifying ourselves mentally and physically, and how to consecrate places and tools.

What is a Witch?

The word we use to define the one who practices witchcraft is Witch. This term comes from the Latin strix, meaning a nocturnal bird of prey. In addition, in Roman religion there was a mythological creature named Strige, also in the guise of a night bird, who was a bad omen and fed on human blood and flesh; she was also a skilled enchantress, able to create evil potions, make predictions and perform metamorphoses from woman to bird. This is why the term "bewitch," meaning to enchant, was born, and hence witch, meaning "enchantress" and "sorceress."

Being a Witch today means practicing magical arts to achieve something, for example, to appease good luck, health, love, healing, or to defend oneself, loved ones, and animals. Being a Witch, however, is a process that starts from within. It is not enough to practice rituals and spells to call oneself one. First, it is necessary to have a deep knowledge of oneself, one's abilities, feelings, and motivations for embarking on this path. This is not something that happens overnight, but through constant daily effort and a strong intentionality to improve oneself consistently. This is all aimed at knowing one's energy. When a Witch knows her energy, she is master of it and can mold it to her will and decide how to use it. In contrast, a Witch who does not know her energy deep down will not know how to control it, and this can make all efforts futile, if not counterproductive.

A Witch then uses her Energy in harmony with the four Elements (Earth, Fire, Air, and Water), with candles, herbs, stones, and more so that it all flows into the realization of the change (or object) she wants. This change can take place in the Witch's life and also in the lives of others, be they relatives, friends, or even people outside her emotional circle. A Witch's intentions for practicing magic can have both positive and negative connotations. As will be reiterated throughout the course of this book, there is no limitation in this except one's conscience. A Witch can decide to act only in Good, as well as only in Evil, or find her balance between the two.

Each individual is made up of Light and Dark, good and bad feelings, and it is the personal decision of the Witch to indulge one or the other or both. One Witch may choose to act only through positive magic as a response to external factors, whatever they may be. In contrast, another may decide to respond to evil inflicted upon her by others by repaying them in the same coin, and this does not make her any less "valid" than the former. There are also those who, like any human being, decide of their own free will to act with evil intent, to pursue the path of Darkness, and this choice makes them Witch in the same way as those who ethically refuse to practice Black Magic. Which path to follow is dictated by your Energy, who you are deep down and what you long for. But remember one thing, practicing magic to make someone else suffer, either physically or mentally, does not make you any better than those who cause harm in the "traditional" way. The fact that spells and rituals are not actionable in the same way as "traditional" violence should not be a reason to cause pain and suffering in an undisturbed and inconspicuous manner.

As mentioned in the introductory chapter, a witch is the one who uses magical and symbolic practices to achieve something, without limits or rules dictated by cults or beliefs. Nothing prohibits you from joining a cult if it is in line with your beliefs and values, but in this case, it is up to you to figure out whether such a cult and Witchcraft can coexist.

No one has the right or the duty to tell you, for example, that you cannot be a Christian and practice Witchcraft. The Bible clearly says that all kinds of magic and witchcraft are prohibited, but no one can forbid you to practice it. In this case, you will be the one to take responsibility for your actions and you will always be accountable for them even before your cult.

Are Witches Born or Become?

This debate has been going on for centuries and will likely never end. Some side with inclusivity, allowing anyone to know themselves and practice according to their own rules. On the other hand, there are those who promote exclusivity and firmly believe that Witches are born, and that it is impossible to learn what is considered an innate gift.

A portion of modern Witches claim that they have come to know Witchcraft through the ancient grimoires bequeathed by their ancestors, within which are enshrined the true principles of Witchcraft handed down through the centuries. For this reason, they believe that only those who own these family grimoires

can be considered full-fledged Witches, as if it were something related to family lineage, and all others would be considered half Witches or fake Witches. Other people claim that to be a Witch, one must possess natural gifts whose presence was manifested at a young age. Some claim to have received their powers through an entity, often a demon, that made them Witches. Still, some simply believe that anyone can practice Witchcraft, as a set of magical and symbolic practices that can be replicated with intent.

But what is the difference? Does it make sense to label oneself in a certain way rather than another, and to justify one's practices through definite reasons?

Granted that everyone is free to believe what he or she most prefers, it is equally unfair to externalize certain considerations if they go to limit or define others and affect their beliefs. What you are or believe you are may be a source of personal pride, but it should not be a reason to belittle those who do not have the same background as you.

It is true, however, that while we can all be Witches, it does not mean we all are. In recent decades, the number of people who call themselves Witches or practitioners of Witchcraft have increased by leaps and bounds, perhaps even out of fashion or leisure. But having a collection of crystals, candles and herbs does not mean you are a Witch. As we discussed at the beginning of this compendium, to practice Witchcraft, one must first have a deep understanding of oneself, nature and the tools used. In short, there must be logic behind everything you do, just as there must be some theoretical knowledge if you have not yet gained practical experience.

Preparing for a Ritual

For a Witch, preparation of oneself and one's space is part of the ritual. In addition to a state of mind in line with the spell or potion you plan to create, you must also prepare yourself physically. Let's see together how.

- **Cleanse and purify**

Just like we prepare for the arrival of guests by cleaning the house to welcome them in the best possible way, we need to energetically cleanse our house and ourselves before practicing any kind of ritual.

To cleanse yourself physically, you can simply wash yourself to remove all the influences and worries of the day. To cleanse your space, proceed by opening the windows and changing the air-in winter. Then you can light a couple of white candles and some incense to purify and give peace and harmony, such as

sandalwood or holy palm. Meditating for a few minutes before starting the ritual can also be very helpful for the ritual's success.

- **_Purifying tools_**

    It is a good idea to purify everything involved in your magical practices. Candles, bottles, and other common objects can be passed through dozens of different hands before they reach you, so you must purify them before using them.

    ◇ *To purify candles and instruments, you can:*
    ◇ *Pass the objects through the smoke of purifying incense;*
    ◇ *Leave objects exposed to the moonlight throughout the night (in this regard, remember that: a full moon is an opening door; a new moon is a closing door; a waxing moon brings energy; a waning moon subtracts energy);*
    ◇ *Wipe the objects with ethyl alcohol;*
    ◇ *Bury the items in a bowl of sea salt for 24 hours.*

- **_Candle dressing_**

    Following candle purification, you can increase the energy of candles by performing candle dressing. Dressing a candle means rubbing on its stem an essential oil suitable for the purpose. If you do not have a specific one available, you can use extra virgin olive oil, which has a neutral action. Some Witches believe that rubbing the candle from top to bottom will attract something to you, while, conversely, rubbing it from the bottom to the top will get rid of something—keep this in mind when dressing your next candle. After that, roll the anointed candle in your favorite dried herbs until it is covered. Of course, you must choose herbs that reinforce your purpose, not randomly. For example, if you want to attract money, you can roll your candle in cinnamon powder. On the other hand, if you want to protect yourself and the places that belong to you, you can roll it in rosemary or thyme.

In this chapter, we discovered what it means to be a Witch, delved into the debate of "being born a Witch" versus "becoming a Witch," and most importantly, learned how to properly prepare ourselves in preparation for a spell or the creation of a magic potion. This chapter also concludes the theoretical part of the compendium. In the next chapter, you will find recipes for creating Witch of Protection Bottles. Now you have all the knowledge to start creating your first bottle, all you have to do is give it a try.

- CHAPTER 4 -

JAR SPELL RECIPES FOR PROTECTION

Protection bottles protect people and places on earthly and occult levels. Several recipes can be prepared according to the purpose. In this chapter we will see how to create Witch's bottles to protect ourselves, our loved ones, our furry friends, places dear to us such as our homes and beyond. In addition, Protection bottles can be aimed at protecting us from evil-doers as well as demons and dark entities, or curses. A word of advice: if you are a beginner, try your hand at the less challenging recipes first. Find the difficulty index at the beginning of each recipe.

Witch Bottle For Personal Protection

 Difficuty
★★

 Preparation Time
5 minutes

 Use
personal protection and that of our loved ones

Ingredients

◇ A small amber glass bottle with cork;
◇ A handful of dried mugwort;
◇ A handful of dried juniper;
◇ A handful of dried rosemary;
◇ A handful of dried thyme;
◇ Pine needles;
◇ 3 strands of black wool 3 cm long;
◇ 3 nails;
◇ 3 rose or cactus thorns (optional);
◇ Moon eclipse water or red wine;
◇ A hair of the person to be protected;
◇ Black or red candle for sealing.

Procedure

1. Insert the hair of the person to be protected into the small bottle. Make sure it got into it and didn't stick to your fingers or the mouth of the bottle - it can happen.
2. Close your eyes and focus for a few seconds on the person for whom the bottle of protection is intended.
3. Insert the needles one at a time, taking care to drop them on the tip, as if you were trying to pierce something.
4. Repeat the process for rose and cactus thorns, being careful to tip them.
5. Now drown the negativity by pouring eclipse moon water or red wine. Caution: if you use powerful liquids such as lunar eclipse water be sure to use only a few drops, otherwise the spell may backfire.
6. Insert the three strands of black wool, one at a time.
7. Mix the five dried herbs (rosemary, thyme, pine needles, juniper, and mugwort), then place the mix in the bottle until it is full or the mixture is finished.
8. Cork the bottle and place it on a protected surface (a saucer, a box, anything you don't mind ruining).
9. Light the candle (possibly black) and wait for the wax to melt.
10. Being careful not to burn yourself, pour melted wax over the cap to seal your witch bottle.
11. Now your bottle is ready. Keep in mind that Saturday is auspicious for the consecration of protection spells, so if possible prefer Saturday to other days to consecrate your protection bottle.

Witch Bottle For House Protection

 *Difficuty* *  *Preparation Time* 5 minutes  *Use* Protection of one's dwelling

Ingredients

◇ A medium-sized amber glass bottle with cork;
◇ A handful of dried rosemary;
◇ 3 needles;
◇ 3 pins;
◇ Red wine;
◇ A black candle for sealing.

Procedure

1. Insert the three needles into the bottle, one at a time, taking care to drop them on the tip as if you were trying to pierce something.
2. Insert the three pins into the bottle, one at a time, again being careful to drop them pointwise.
3. Cover the needles and pins with dried rosemary.
4. Fill with red wine to drown out negativity and bad influences.
5. Cork the bottle and place it on a protected surface (a saucer, a box, anything you don't mind ruining).
6. Light the candle (black or red) and wait for the wax to melt.
7. Being careful not to burn yourself, pour melted wax over the cap to seal your witch bottle.
8. Now your bottle is ready. Keep in mind that Saturday is auspicious for the consecration of protection spells, so if possible prefer Saturday to other days to consecrate your protection bottle.
9. Bury the protection bottle in the farthest corner of your property to allow the spell to keep negative influences as far away from you and your home as possible.
10. If you bury it in the ground, you can draw a pentagram in the earth above the bottle to increase the power of the protection spell.
11. If you live in an apartment, you can opt to hide the protective bottle in the house, but be careful to put it in a place that is not visible or accessible to others.

Witch's Bottle For The Protection Of Spaces

 Difficuty
＊

 Preparation Time
5 minutes

 Use
Protect your own space outside your home (e.g., the office where you work)

Ingredients

◇ A medium-sized dark glass bottle with a cork;
◇ 7 nails, preferably old and rusty;
◇ 1 teaspoon dried rosemary;
◇ A handful of black salt;
◇ A black candle for sealing.

Procedure

1. Insert the seven needles into the bottle, one at a time, taking care to drop them on the tip as if you were trying to pierce something.
2. Cover the needles with dried rosemary.
3. Cover with black salt.
4. Cork the bottle and place it on a protected surface (a saucer, a box, anything you don't mind ruining).
5. Light the black candle and wait for the wax to melt a little.
6. Being careful not to burn yourself, pour melted wax over the cap to seal your witch bottle.
7. Now your bottle is ready. Keep in mind that Saturday is auspicious for the consecration of protection spells, so if possible prefer Saturday to other days to consecrate your protection bottle.
8. Hide the protection bottle in the room you want to protect, but be careful to put it in a place that is not visible or accessible to others.

Witch's Bottle For The Protection Of One's Animals

 *Difficuty*
★ ★

 *Preparation Time*
5 minutes

 *Use*
Pet and non-pet protection

Ingredients

◊ A medium-sized dark glass bottle with a cork;
◊ A hair of the animal;
◊ A paper card;
◊ Pen;
◊ 3 ivy leaves;
◊ A handful of catnip;
◊ A handful of dried Rosemary;
◊ Brown candle (animal propitiation) for sealing.

Procedure

1. Insert the animal hair into the bottle (be careful that it has fallen to the bottom and not stuck to your fingers or the neck of the bottle-it can happen);
2. Write your pet's name on the slip of paper, then roll the slip of paper up like a tiny parchment and drop it inside the bottle;
3. Insert a pinch of dried rosemary into the bottle;
4. Insert the three ivy leaves into the bottle, one at a time, taking care that they do not break in the process;
5. Insert a handful of catnip into the bottle.
6. Cork the bottle and place it on a protected surface (a saucer, a box, anything you don't mind ruining).
7. Light the brown candle and wait for the wax to melt a little.
8. Being careful not to burn yourself, pour melted wax over the cap to seal your witch bottle.
9. Now your bottle is ready. Keep in mind that Saturday is auspicious for the consecration of protection spells, so if possible prefer Saturday to other days to consecrate your protection bottle.
10. Hide the bottle in a place your pet frequents a lot, such as where his or her kennel is, but be careful to hide it out of sight and, most importantly, in a place where it will not be touched or moved by anyone but you;
11. If, on the other hand, you created the protection bottle to protect your farm animals, you can opt to bury the bottle in a corner of the pen, barn, chicken coop or place where you keep your animals safe.

Witch Bottle For The Protection Of Children And Infants

 *Difficuty* ★    *Preparation Time* 5 minutes    *Use* protection of children and infants from negative influences

Ingredients

◊ A medium-sized dark glass bottle with a cork;
◊ A handful of hawthorn berries;
◊ Anise;
◊ Basil leaves;
◊ A sprig of acacia;
◊ Pen;
◊ Paper sheet;
◊ White candle for sealing;

Procedure

1. Write on the slip of paper the name of the child you want to protect, then roll the slip of paper up like a tiny parchment and drop it inside the bottle;
2. Insert a handful of star anise into the bottle;
3. Insert the acacia sprig into the bottle;
4. Insert hawthorn berries into the bottle, one at a time;
5. Insert the basil leaves into the bottle, one at a time, taking care that they do not break in the process;
6. Cork the bottle and place it on a protected surface (a saucer, a box, anything you don't mind ruining).
7. Light the white candle and wait for the wax to melt a little.
8. Being careful not to burn yourself, pour melted wax over the cap to seal your witch bottle.
9. Now your bottle is ready. Keep in mind that Saturday is auspicious for the consecration of protection spells, so if possible prefer Saturday to other days to consecrate your protection bottle.
10. Hide the bottle in the child's room for whom you intended the spell, but be very careful to hide it away from the sight of others and, above all, in a place where it will not be touched or moved by anyone but you.

Witch's Bottle For Negative Vibes

 *Difficuty* ✱

 *Preparation Time* 5 minutes + 24 hours

 *Use* check for negative vibrations within a confined environment

Ingredients

◇ A medium-sized container made of clear glass;
◇ Coarse salt;
◇ Apple vinegar.

Procedure

1. Place three tablespoons of coarse salt in the clear glass container;
2. Cover the salt with apple cider vinegar until it almost fills the container;
3. Place the container in the room of your choice, preferably in a corner, and make sure no one moves it from there or touches it for the next twenty-four hours.
4. After twenty-four hours have passed, check the state of the salt. If nothing has changed, the chosen environment is not permeated with negative vibrations, so you can simply move the container to another room and repeat the process.
5. If, on the other hand, the salt has risen to the surface, climbing the walls of the container, it has activated its power to absorb negative energies. In this case flush the mixture down the toilet and rinse the container very well before repeating the process in another room. To clean a room permeated with negative energies you can use palo santo or white sage, open windows wide to make air exchange and clean floors and surfaces with water and coarse salt.
6. If the salt has taken on a strange color (often greenish) there is likely a curse or the presence of some dark entity. In this case you will have to proceed with purification of the room.

Bottle Of The Witch For The Protection Of The Family

 Difficuty
★

 Preparation Time
5 minutes

 Use
protecting the family

Ingredients

- A medium-sized dark glass bottle with a cork;
- A photo depicting all family members together;
- Coarse salt;
- Pen or marker;
- Disinfectant;
- White tape;
- Hawthorn berries;
- A sprig of acacia;
- White candle for sealing;

Procedure

1. Write the name of each family member next to his or her head (including animals) on the photograph.
2. Roll up the photograph, fasten it with white ribbon, and then stick it in the bottle.
3. Insert the acacia sprig into the bottle;
4. Insert hawthorn berries into the bottle, one at a time.
5. Insert a drop of disinfectant for each family member, visualizing healing each of their wounds.
6. Fill the bottle with rock salt.
7. Cork the bottle and place it on a protected surface (a saucer, a box, anything you don't mind ruining).
8. Light the white candle and wait for the wax to melt a little.
9. Being careful not to burn yourself, pour melted wax over the cap to seal your witch bottle.
10. Now your bottle is ready. Keep in mind that Saturday is auspicious for the consecration of protection spells, so if possible prefer Saturday to other days to consecrate your protection bottle.
11. Hide the bottle near the entrance gate of your property. If you live in an apartment, find a place near the front door, but be careful that it is not visible or reachable by anyone, especially pets and children.

Witch's Bottle To Protect The House From Spirits

 Difficuty
★

 Preparation Time
5 minutes

 Use
to protect the house from evil spirits and presences

Ingredients

◇ Four small dark glass bottles with corks;
◇ A handful of dried St. John's Wort;
◇ A handful of dried dill;
◇ A handful of dried verbena;
◇ Lavender essential oil;
◇ Dried rose petals;
◇ 12 pins;
◇ White candle for sealing;

Procedure

1. Carry out candle dressing first by massaging the candle with lavender essential oil from the center upward (drive out, away) and then rolling it in dried rose petals;
2. Insert dried St. John's Wort into the bottles;
3. Insert the dried dill into the bottles;
4. Insert dried verbena into the bottles;
5. Insert three pins for each bottle, one at a time, and drop them pointwise (as if you were trying to stab something).
6. Place one drop of lavender essential oil in each small bottle;
7. Cork the bottles and place them on a protected surface (a saucer, a box, anything you don't mind ruining).
8. Light the white candle and wait for the wax to melt a little.
9. Being careful not to burn yourself, pour melted wax over the cap to seal your witch bottles.
10. Now your protection bottles are at the ready. Keep in mind that Saturday is auspicious for the consecration of protection spells, so if possible prefer Saturday to other days to consecrate your protection bottles.
11. Hide the bottles in the four corners of the house, in a hidden place unreachable by others.

THE JAR SPELLS   33

Witch's Bottle For Protection From The Envy Of Others

 *Difficuty*  *Preparation Time*  *Use*

★ 5 minutes protecting oneself from others' envy

Ingredients

◊ A small, dark glass bottle with a cork;
◊ A picture of you;
◊ Coarse salt;
◊ White silk ribbon;
◊ Pen;
◊ Paper sheet;
◊ White candle for sealing;

Procedure

1.
2.
3. Procedure:
4. Roll up your photo and close it with the white silk ribbon;
5. Insert the photo into the bottle;
6. Insert three grains of coarse salt into the bottle;
7. On a card write the following formula: "Let any wrong or evil addressed to me be shielded by this bottle."
8. Roll up the card like a scroll and insert it into the bottle;
9. Cork the bottle and place it on a protected surface (a saucer, a box, anything you don't mind ruining).
10. Light the white candle and wait for the wax to melt a little.
11. Being careful not to burn yourself, pour melted wax over the cap to seal your witch bottle.
12. Now your bottle is ready. Keep in mind that Saturday is auspicious for the consecration of protection spells, so if possible prefer Saturday to other days to consecrate your protection bottle.
13. Carry your bottle with you, in a pocket or purse. You mustn't let anyone touch your protection bottle. The power of this protection bottle runs out every three months, so to stay protected create another one. You can only recycle your photo from the old bottle, all other ingredients must be replaced and the old contents burned

Witch's Bottle To Protect Oneself From Misfortune

 *Difficuty* ★ ★ ★  *Preparation Time* 60 minutes  *Use* to protect oneself from misfortune

Ingredients

◇ A medium-sized dark glass bottle with a cork;
◇ 100 red rose petals;
◇ Freshly picked moss;
◇ Oregano;
◇ Holy water (or disinfectant);
◇ Mortar and pestle;
◇ White candle for sealing;

Procedure

1. Peel off 100 red rose petals and place them in a container of holy water for one hour.
2. After an hour has elapsed, remove the petals from the holy water, put them in a mortar and pound to make a juice.
3. Pour the resulting juice into the bottle.
4. Insert moss into the bottle.
5. Place a handful of oregano in the bottle.
6. Cork the bottle and place it on a protected surface (a saucer, a box, anything you don't mind ruining).
7. Light the white candle and wait for the wax to melt a little.
8. Being careful not to burn yourself, pour melted wax over the cap to seal your witch bottle.
9. Now your bottle is ready. Keep in mind that Saturday is auspicious for the consecration of protection spells, so if possible prefer Saturday to other days to consecrate your protection bottle.
10. Hold the bottle under your bed until the color of the mixture changes color. When this happens it means the bottle has done its job, so undo it.

Witch's Bottle To Protect Against Negative Influences

 *Difficulty*
★

 *Preparation Time*
10 minutes

 *Use*
Protection from negative influences

Ingredients

- A medium-sized amber glass bottle with cork;
- A handful of dried rosemary;
- Galbanum sprig;
- Lavender sprig;
- Needles or pins;
- Nettles;
- Olive leaves;
- A white candle for sealing.

Procedure

1. Insert the dried rosemary into the bottle.
2. Insert the galbanum sprig and the lavender sprig into the bottle.
3. Insert three pins into the bottle, one at a time, and drop them pointwise (as if you were trying to stick something).
4. Insert a handful of nettles (possibly using a glove).
5. Cork the bottle and place it on a protected surface (a saucer, a box, anything you don't mind ruining).
6. Light the white candle and wait for the wax to melt a little.
7. Being careful not to burn yourself, pour melted wax over the cap to seal your witch bottle.
8. Now your bottle is ready. Keep in mind that Saturday is auspicious for the consecration of protection spells, so if possible prefer Saturday to other days to consecrate your protection bottle.
9. Keep the bottle with you always in your pocket or purse.

Witch Bottle For Protection From Thieves

Difficuty
*

Preparation Time
10 minutes

Use
to protect against thieves and theft

Ingredients

◊ A medium-sized amber glass bottle with cork;
◊ Amethyst chips;
◊ Juniper berries;
◊ Red wine;
◊ Rosemary sprig;
◊ Monetines;
◊ Padlock;
◊ A white candle for sealing.

Procedure

1. Insert rosemary into the bottle.
2. Pour the amethyst chips into the bottle.
3. Insert the padlock into the bottle (it must be locked and keyless).
4. Insert the coins, one at a time.
5. Insert juniper berries;
6. Pour red wine until the bottle is full.
7. Cork the bottle and place it on a protected surface (a saucer, a box, anything you don't mind ruining).
8. Light the white candle and wait for the wax to melt a little.
9. Being careful not to burn yourself, pour melted wax over the cap to seal your witch bottle.
10. Now your bottle is ready. Keep in mind that Saturday is auspicious for the consecration of protection spells, so if possible prefer Saturday to other days to consecrate your protection bottle.
11. Keep the bottle with you always in your pocket or purse.

THE JAR SPELLS

Witch's Bottle To Protect Oneself From Assailants

Difficuty
★★

Preparation Time
10 minutes

Use
to protect oneself from malicious attackers

Ingredients

◇ A medium-sized amber glass bottle with cork;
◇ A handful of dried mugwort;
◇ A handful of dried rosemary;
◇ A handful of euphorbia;
◇ Amethyst;
◇ 3 nails;
◇ Moon eclipse water;
◇ Black or red candle for sealing.

Procedure

1. Insert the rosemary and mugwort into the bottle.
2. Insert the amethyst into the bottle.
3. Insert juniper berries and euphorbia.
4. Pour ten drops of eclipse moon water.
5. Insert three rusty nails.
6. Cork the bottle and place it on a protected surface (a saucer, a box, anything you don't mind ruining).
7. Light the white candle and wait for the wax to melt a little.
8. Being careful not to burn yourself, pour melted wax over the cap to seal your witch bottle.
9. Now your bottle is ready. Keep in mind that Saturday is auspicious for the consecration of protection spells, so if possible prefer Saturday to other days to consecrate your protection bottle.
10. Keep the bottle with you always in your pocket or purse.

Witch's Bottle of Generic Protection

Difficuty
*

Preparation Time
10 minutes

Use
Attracting good fortune in business

Ingredients
◇ A medium-sized amber glass bottle with cork;
◇ Rosemary sprig;
◇ Coffee grounds;
◇ Tiger eye chips;
◇ Parsley;
◇ Lavender essential oil;
◇ White candle for sealing.

Procedure
1. Insert coffee grounds into the bottle.
2. Pour in the fresh parsley.
3. Pour in the tiger eye chips.
4. Add a few drops of lavender essential oil.
5. Insert the rosemary sprig.
6. Cork the bottle and place it on a protected surface (a saucer, a box, anything you don't mind ruining).
7. Light the white candle and wait for the wax to melt a little.
8. Being careful not to burn yourself, pour melted wax over the cap to seal your witch bottle.
9. Now your bottle is ready. Keep in mind that Saturday is auspicious for the consecration of protection spells, so if possible prefer Saturday to other days to consecrate your protection bottle.
10. Keep the bottle with you at all times or in the room where you spend most of your time.

Witch's Bottle To Protect One's Memories

Difficuty
★

Preparation Time
10 minutes

Use
protecting memories and memory

Ingredients

◊ A medium-sized amber glass bottle with cork;
◊ Artemisia;
◊ Poppy seeds;
◊ Elderflower;
◊ Adularia (moonstone);
◊ Full moon water;
◊ Silver candle for sealing.

Procedure

1. Insert the poppy seeds into the bottle, one at a time.
2. Insert adularia into the bottle.
3. Add mugwort and elderflower.
4. Add a few drops of full moon water.
5. Cork the bottle and place it on a protected surface (a saucer, a box, anything you don't mind ruining).
6. Light the silver candle and wait for the wax to melt a little.
7. Being careful not to burn yourself, pour melted wax over the cap to seal your witch bottle.
8. Now your bottle is ready. Keep in mind that Saturday is auspicious for the consecration of protection spells, so if possible prefer Saturday to other days to consecrate your protection bottle.
9. Keep the bottle with you at all times or under your pillow.
10.

Witch Bottle To Protect Against Accidents

Difficuty
★ ★

Preparation Time
10 minutes

Use
protecting yourself from accidents

Ingredients

◇ A medium-sized amber glass bottle with cork;
◇ Onion;
◇ Rosemary sprig;
◇ Jade chips;
◇ Black salt;
◇ Sunshine water;
◇ Yellow candle for sealing.

Procedure

1. Cut the onion in half and insert it into the bottle.
2. Pour in the jade chips, one at a time.
3. Add black salt, one grain at a time. As you do this, visualize the salt grains building your invisible armor against accidents.
4. Add a few drops of sun water.
5. Insert the rosemary sprig into the bottle.
6. Cork the bottle and place it on a protected surface (a saucer, a box, anything you don't mind ruining).
7. Light the yellow candle and wait for the wax to melt a little.
8. Being careful not to burn yourself, pour melted wax over the cap to seal your witch bottle.
9. Now your bottle is ready. Keep in mind that Saturday is auspicious for the consecration of protection spells, so if possible prefer Saturday to other days to consecrate your protection bottle.
10. Keep the bottle with you at all times or, if you own a car or other vehicle, keep it under the driver's seat.

Witch's Bottle To Protect Oneself From The Evil Eye

Difficuty
★★★

Preparation Time
10 minutes

Use
to protect oneself from the evil eye

Ingredients

- A medium-sized amber glass bottle with cork;
- Hyssop sprig;
- Viburnum sprig;
- Amethyst chips;
- Rose thorns;
- Lavender essential oil;
- Purple candle for sealing.

Procedure

1. Insert the sprig of hyssop into the bottle.
2. Insert the viburnum sprig into the bottle.
3. Pour in the amethyst chips, one at a time.
4. Add rose thorns, one at a time. As you do this, visualize that each thorn is protecting you from the evil eye like an armor.
5. Add three drops of lavender essential oil.
6. Cork the bottle and place it on a protected surface (a saucer, a box, anything you don't mind ruining).
7. Light the yellow candle and wait for the wax to melt a little.
8. Being careful not to burn yourself, pour melted wax over the cap to seal your witch bottle.
9. Now your bottle is ready. Keep in mind that Saturday is auspicious for the consecration of protection spells, so if possible prefer Saturday to other days to consecrate your protection bottle.
10. Keep the bottle with you always and don't let anyone touch it.

Witch Bottle To Protect Beauty

Difficuty
★ ★

Preparation Time
10 minutes

Use
to protect one's beauty and youthfulness

Ingredients

◇ A small amber glass bottle with a cork;
◇ Dried rose petals;
◇ Dried hibiscus flowers;
◇ Galangal root;
◇ Sapphire chips;
◇ Lavender essential oil;
◇ Purple candle for sealing.

Procedure

1. Place rose petals and dried hibiscus flowers in the bottle.
2. Insert the galangal root into the bottle.
3. Pour in the sapphire chips, one at a time.
4. Add three drops of lavender essential oil.
5. Cork the bottle and place it on a protected surface (a saucer, a box, anything you don't mind ruining).
6. Light the purple candle and wait for the wax to melt a little.
7. Being careful not to burn yourself, pour melted wax over the cap to seal your witch bottle.
8. Now your bottle is ready. Keep in mind that Saturday is auspicious for the consecration of protection spells, so if possible prefer Saturday to other days to consecrate your protection bottle.
9. Keep the bottle with you always and don't let anyone touch it.

Witch Bottle To Protect Plants

Difficuty ★★

Preparation Time 10 minutes

Use protecting plants

Ingredients

◊ A small amber glass bottle with a cork;
◊ A handful of fertile soil;
◊ Cinnamon powder;
◊ Coffee beans;
◊ Jade chips;
◊ Full moon water;
◊ Green or brown candle for sealing.

Procedure

1. Insert the coffee beans into the bottle.
2. Insert fertile soil into the bottle.
3. Add jade chips and cinnamon powder.
4. Add a few drops of full moon water;
5. Cork the bottle and place it on a protected surface (a saucer, a box, anything you don't mind ruining).
6. Light the green candle and wait for the wax to melt a little.
7. Being careful not to burn yourself, pour melted wax over the cap to seal your witch bottle.
8. Now your bottle is ready. Keep in mind that Saturday is auspicious for the consecration of protection spells, so if possible prefer Saturday to other days to consecrate your protection bottle.
9. Bury the bottle in the pot of the plant to be protected. You can also bury it in the garden or vegetable garden, but it is advisable to make more than one by burying them in the corners of the garden.

Witch Bottle To Protect Oneself From Addiction

Difficuty
★ ★

Preparation Time
10 minutes

Use
protecting oneself from addiction

Ingredients

- A small amber glass bottle with a cork;
- Blueberries;
- Ivy leaves;
- Holy thistle;
- Red wine;
- Aloe vera;
- Eucalyptus;
- Purple candle for sealing.

Procedure

1. Insert the blueberries into the bottle, one at a time.
2. Insert ivy and holy thistle into the bottle.
3. Insert a slice of aloe vera into the bottle.
4. Add eucalyptus.
5. Fill the bottle with red wine.
6. Cork the bottle and place it on a protected surface (a saucer, a box, anything you don't mind ruining).
7. Light the purple candle and wait for the wax to melt a little.
8. Being careful not to burn yourself, pour melted wax over the cap to seal your witch bottle.
9. Now your bottle is ready. Keep in mind that Saturday is auspicious for the consecration of protection spells, so if possible prefer Saturday to other days to consecrate your protection bottle.
10. Keep the bottle with you always and do not let anyone touch it.

- CHAPTER 5 -

Jar Spell Recipes To Attract Love

Bottles to attract Love have different purposes and varying degrees of intensity. They can be used to cause infatuation, to appease the meeting of true love, to heal a troubled relationship, to bring back one or an ex, to foster family affection and love, and more. Several recipes can be prepared according to the purpose. In this chapter we will see how to create Witch bottles to attract love in all its forms. A word of advice: if you are a beginner, try your hand at the less challenging recipes first. Find the difficulty index at the beginning of each recipe.

Witch Bottle To Attract Passionate Love

Difficuty
★★

Preparation Time
15 minutes

Use
Attracting passionate love

Ingredients

- A medium-sized dark glass bottle with a cork;
- Sugar;
- A handful of dried coriander;
- Cinnamon sticks;
- Dried red rose petals;
- Paper sheet;
- Pen;
- Red candle for sealing.

Procedure

1. Begin the ritual with ten minutes of meditation. Think intensely about your ideal partner, the sensations it causes you, and imagine how you would feel if you were already in the company of your dream partner.
2. Insert three dried red rose petals into the bottle, careful not to break them.
3. Insert a few pinches of dried coriander into the bottle;
4. Insert three cinnamon sticks, one at a time.
5. Take a piece of paper and write down in one sentence what is most important to you in a passionate relationship.
6. Roll the paper up like a small parchment and insert it into the bottle.
7. Pour a few pinches of sugar into the bottle.
8. Cork the bottle and place it on a protected surface (a saucer, a box, anything you don't mind ruining).
9. Light the red candle and wait for the wax to melt a little. In the meantime you can close your eyes again and think hard about your intentions.
10. Being careful not to burn yourself, pour melted wax over the cap to seal your witch bottle.
11. Now your bottle is ready. Remember that Tuesday is auspicious for love and passion spells, so if possible prefer Tuesday to other days to consecrate your love bottle.
12. Hide the bottle away from the view of others and, most importantly, in a place where it will not be touched or moved by anyone.

THE JAR SPELLS

Bottle Of The Witch To Attract Eternal Love

Difficuty
★ ★ ★

Preparation Time
15 minutes

Use
Attracting passionate love

Ingredients

◊ A medium-sized dark glass bottle with a cork;
◊ Organic honey;
◊ Dried white and rose petals;
◊ Paper sheet;
◊ Pen;
◊ Rose quartz (rough is best);
◊ Pink Himalayan salt;
◊ Pink candle for sealing.

Procedure

1. Begin the ritual with ten minutes of meditation. Think intensely about your ideal partner, the sensations it causes you, and imagine how you would feel if you were already in the company of your dream partner.
2. Place three dried white (or rose) rose petals in the bottle, careful not to break them.
3. Insert a few pinches of pink Himalayan salt into the bottle.
4. Place rose quartz in the bottle (rough is best, but you can also use a tumbled stone as long as it has been purified beforehand).
5. Take a piece of paper and write in one sentence the most important aspect of a lasting relationship to you.
6. Roll the leaflet up like a small parchment, dip it generously in organic honey, and then insert it into the bottle.
7. Cork the bottle and place it on a protected surface (a saucer, a box, anything you don't mind ruining).
8. Light the pink candle and wait for the wax to melt a little. In the meantime you can close your eyes again and think hard about your intentions.
9. Being careful not to burn yourself, pour melted wax over the cap to seal your witch bottle.
10. Now your bottle is ready. Remember that Tuesday is auspicious for love and passion spells, so if possible prefer Tuesday to other days to consecrate your love bottle.
11. Hide the bottle away from the view of others and, most importantly, in a place where it will not be touched or moved by anyone.

Witch Bottle To Attract A Particular Person

Difficuty
★ ★ ★
★ ★

Preparation Time
20 minutes

Use
Attracting a specific person to oneself

Warning: this spell may fall under Black Magic, as you are forcing the will of another individual. Make sure that the person you want to attract has feelings toward you. Otherwise, the attraction you would cause in the other person would only be fictitious.

Ingredients

◇ A medium-sized dark glass bottle with a cork;
◇ Rose essential oil;
◇ Garlic clove;
◇ Photo of loved one;
◇ A picture of you;
◇ Pen and paper;
◇ Raw ruby chips;
◇ A handful of cilantro;
◇ Red candle for sealing.

1. Begin the ritual with ten minutes of meditation. Think intensely about the person you have chosen, the feelings you get from having that person near you, and imagine how you would feel if you were already a couple;
2. Insert raw ruby chips into the bottle, thinking or saying aloud, "These stones symbolize the fragments of your heart that belong to me, now and forever."
3. Insert the garlic clove into the bottle.
4. Take a piece of paper and write your and your partner's names, then circle them both closed. Finally pour a drop of rose essential oil on it.
5. Roll the paper up like a small parchment and insert it into the bottle.
6. Enter your partner's photo, then your own.
7. Insert a few pinches of cilantro into the bottle.
8. Cork the bottle and place it on a protected surface (a saucer, a box, anything you don't mind ruining).
9. Light the red candle and wait for the wax to melt a little. In the meantime, you can close your eyes again and think intensely about your partner. To make the candle's effect even more powerful, you can preemptively go ahead and do a dressing by steeping it in rose essential oil and then rolling it in a mixture of cinnamon, rose petals and chamomile.
10. Being careful not to burn yourself, pour melted wax over the cap to seal your witch bottle.
11. Now your bottle is ready. Remember that Tuesday is auspicious for love and passion spells, so if possible prefer Tuesday to other days to consecrate your love bottle.
12. Hide the bottle away from the view of others and, most importantly, in a place where it will not be touched or moved by anyone.

Witch Bottle To Bring An Ex Back

Difficuty ★★★★

Preparation Time 20 minutes

Use Attracting an ex to himself

Warning: this spell may fall under Black Magic, as you are forcing the will of another individual. Make sure that the person you want to bring back still has positive feelings for you. Otherwise, the attraction you would cause in the other person would only be fictitious and could be counterproductive.

Ingredients

◇ A medium-sized dark glass bottle with a cork;
◇ Orange blossom;
◇ Devil's claw;
◇ A handful of dried coriander;
◇ Photos of you and your ex(es) together (if you don't have one you can make a collage of two photos or insert a photo of you and a photo of your partner separately);
◇ Pen and paper;
◇ Rough rose quartz chips;
◇ Red candle for sealing.

1. Begin the ritual with ten minutes of meditation. Think intensely about your ex, the feelings of having that person near you, and imagine how you would feel if you were a couple again;
2. Insert orange blossoms into the bottle.
3. Insert devil's claw into the bottle.
4. Take a piece of paper and write your and your partner's names, then circle them both closed.
5. Roll the paper up like a small parchment and insert it into the bottle.
6. Enter your photo (if you don't have one, enter your ex's first and then your own).
7. Insert a few pinches of dried coriander into the bottle;
8. Insert raw rose quartz chips into the bottle, thinking or saying aloud, "These stones symbolize the fragments of your heart that belong to me, now and forever. By inserting them into this bottle I command you to return to me."
9. Cork the bottle and place it on a protected surface (a saucer, a box, anything you don't mind ruining).
10. Light the pink candle and wait for the wax to melt a little. In the meantime, you can close your eyes and think hard about the rapprochement between you and your ex. To make the candle's effect even more powerful, you can preemptively go ahead and do a dressing by steeping it in rose essential oil and then rolling it in a mixture of cinnamon, rose petals and coriander.
11. Being careful not to burn yourself, pour melted wax over the cap to seal your witch bottle.
12. Now your bottle is ready. Remember that Tuesday is auspicious for love and passion spells, so if possible prefer Tuesday to other days to consecrate your love bottle.
13. Hide the bottle away from the view of others and, most importantly, in a place where it will not be touched or moved by anyone.

Witch's Bottle to Strengthen an Extinguished Love.

Difficuty
★★★

Preparation Time
10 minutes

Use
Strengthening a pre-existing love

Ingredients

◇ A medium-sized dark glass bottle with a cork;
◇ Orange ribbon or thread;
◇ Couple photos;
◇ Chamomile flowers;
◇ Dehydrated orange peels;
◇ Lavender sprig;
◇ A sprig of rosemary;
◇ Organic honey;
◇ Pink candle for sealing.

Procedure

1. Begin the ritual with ten minutes of meditation. Think intensely about your partner, the feelings of having him or her near you, and imagine how you would feel if you were a happy, close-knit couple again;
2. Insert the orange peels into the bottle.
3. Insert your photo taken at a very happy moment into the bottle.
4. Insert the rosemary sprig and the lavender sprig into the bottle.
5. Insert the orange ribbon into the bottle.
6. Cover all the ingredients with organic honey. As you do this think or recite aloud the words, "Let this honey be the glue that brings us together never to be lost again."
7. Cork the bottle and place it on a protected surface (a saucer, a box, anything you don't mind ruining).
8. Light the pink candle and wait for the wax to melt a little. In the meantime you can close your eyes and think hard about the rapprochement between you and your partner. Being careful not to burn yourself pour the melted wax over the cap to seal your witch bottle.
9. Now your bottle is ready. Remember that Tuesday is auspicious for love and passion spells, so if possible prefer Tuesday to other days to consecrate your love bottle.
10. Hide the bottle away from the view of others and, most importantly, in a place where it will not be touched or moved by anyone.

Witch Bottle To Seduce Someone

Difficuty
★ ★ ★

Preparation Time
10 minutes

Use
Seducing someone

Ingredients

◊ A medium-sized dark glass bottle with a cork;
◊ Garlic;
◊ A handful of dried coriander;
◊ A sprig of heather;
◊ Red ribbon;
◊ Red wine;
◊ Red rose petals;
◊ Red candle for sealing.

Procedure

1. Insert three cloves of garlic into the bottle.
2. Insert a handful of dried cilantro into the bottle.
3. Insert the rosemary sprig and the lavender sprig into the bottle.
4. Insert the red ribbon into the bottle.
5. Insert the red rose petals into the bottle, ensuring they do not break during the procedure.
6. Insert heather sprig.
7. Pour red wine until the bottle is half full.
8. Cork the bottle and place it on a protected surface (a saucer, a box, anything you don't mind ruining).
9. Light the red candle and wait for the wax to melt a little.
10. Being careful not to burn yourself, pour melted wax over the cap to seal your witch bottle.
11. Now your bottle is ready. Remember that Tuesday is auspicious for love and passion spells, so if possible prefer Tuesday to other days to consecrate your love bottle.
12. Hide the bottle away from the view of others and, most importantly, in a place where it will not be touched or moved by anyone.

Witch Bottle To Attract Eternal Love

Difficuty
★ ★ ★ ★

Preparation Time
30 minutes

Use
Attracting eternal love

Ingredients

◊ A medium-sized dark glass bottle with a cork;
◊ Red ribbon;
◊ Orchid not yet cut;
◊ Petals of beauty at night;
◊ Red or pink glitter;
◊ Snowflake;
◊ A natural pearl;
◊ Three drops of seawater;
◊ Pink rose petals;
◊ Absinthe;
◊ Pink candle for sealing.

Procedure

1. Insert petals of night beauty into the bottle.
2. Insert the natural pearl into the bottle.
3. Insert the red ribbon into the bottle.
4. Insert the pink rose petals into the bottle, ensuring they do not break off during the procedure.
5. Insert glitter, neither too much nor too little.
6. Recut an orchid flower, the most beautiful on the plant, with disinfected scissors and insert it into the bottle.
7. Pour in absinthe until the bottle is filled.
8. Pour in the three drops of seawater.
9. Have a snowflake fall naturally inside (do not pick it up).
10. Close the bottle with the cork, shake it so the glitter spreads into the liquid, and place it on a protected surface (a saucer, a box, anything you don't mind ruining).
11. Light the pink candle and wait for the wax to melt a little.
12. Being careful not to burn yourself, pour melted wax over the cap to seal your witch bottle.
13. Now your bottle is ready. Remember that Tuesday is auspicious for love and passion spells, so if possible prefer Tuesday to other days to consecrate your love bottle.
14. Hide the bottle away from the view of others and, most importantly, in a place where it will not be touched or moved by anyone.
15. When you find your soul mate get rid of the witch's bottle in a freshwater stream.

THE JAR SPELLS

Witch Bottle To Increase Fertility

Difficuty
★ ★ ★

Preparation Time
10 minutes

Use
to increase fertility and propitiate pregnancy

Ingredients

◇ A medium-sized dark glass bottle with a cork;
◇ Carnelian;
◇ Hawthorn berries;
◇ Wood fern;
◇ Mandrake root;
◇ Peach blossom;
◇ Rose water;
◇ Pink candle for sealing.

Procedure

1. Insert hawthorn berries into the bottle.
2. Insert the carnelian into the bottle.
3. Insert mandrake root and wood fern into the bottle.
4. Pour two drops of rosewater on the peach blossom, then place the latter in the bottle.
5. Cork the bottle and place it on a protected surface (a saucer, a box, anything you don't mind ruining).
6. Light the pink candle and wait for the wax to melt a little.
7. Being careful not to burn yourself, pour melted wax over the cap to seal your witch bottle.
8. Now your bottle is ready. Keep in mind that Tuesday is auspicious for love and passion spells, so if possible prefer Tuesday to other days to consecrate your love bottle.
9. Hide the bottle in the bedroom, preferably under the mattress

Witch's Bottle To Avert Betrayal

Difficuty ★★

Preparation Time 30 minutes

Use Avoiding amorous betrayals

Ingredients

◇ A medium-sized dark glass bottle with a cork;
◇ Licorice;
◇ Nutmeg;
◇ Yellow rose petals;
◇ Wolfsbane leaves;
◇ Blueberry leaves;
◇ Pen and paper;
◇ Red candle for sealing.

Procedure

1. Collect aconite leaves, yellow rose petals and blueberry leaves in a fireproof container. Burn the herbs and collect the ashes.
2. Once the ashes have cooled, pour them into the bottle.
3. Insert three licorice sticks into the bottle.
4. Write your name and your loved one's name on a sheet of paper, then draw a circle around the two names. Insert the folded paper into the bottle.
5. Sprinkle some nutmeg powder into the bottle.
6. Cork the bottle by placing it on a protected surface (a saucer, a box, anything you don't mind ruining).
7. Light the pink candle and wait for the wax to melt a little.
8. Being careful not to burn yourself, pour melted wax over the cap to seal your witch bottle.
9. Now your bottle is ready. Keep in mind that Tuesday is auspicious for love and passion spells, so if possible prefer Tuesday to other days to consecrate your love bottle.
10. Hide the bottle under your loved one's mattress (or side of the bed).

Witch's Bottle For Loving Yourself

Difficuty
★

Preparation Time
10 minutes

Use
loving oneself

Ingredients

◇ A medium-sized dark glass bottle with a cork;
◇ Pink salt;
◇ Pink rose petals;
◇ Rose quartz;
◇ Dragon's blood (resin);
◇ Rose water;
◇ Pink candle for sealing.

Procedure

1. Fill the bottle halfway with pink salt.
2. Insert rose quartz;
3. Add rose petals;
4. Add a teaspoon of dragon's blood;
5. Fill the bottle with rosewater;
6. Cork the bottle by placing it on a protected surface (a saucer, a box, anything you don't mind ruining).
7. Light the pink candle and wait for the wax to melt a little.
8. Being careful not to burn yourself, pour melted wax over the cap to seal your witch bottle.
9. Now your bottle is ready. Keep in mind that Tuesday is auspicious for love and passion spells, so if possible prefer Tuesday to other days to consecrate your love bottle.
10. Keep the bottle with you at all times.

Witch Bottle to Foster Couple Communication.

Difficuty
★

Preparation Time
10 minutes

Use
to propitiate couple communication and mutual understanding

Ingredients

◇ A small, dark glass bottle with a cork;
◇ Sodalite chips;
◇ Rose petals;
◇ Cornflower;
◇ Full moon water;
◇ Pink candle for sealing.

Procedure

1. Fill the bottle halfway with the sodalite chips.
2. Fill the remaining half of the bottle with rose petals and cornflower;
3. Add a few drops of full moon water (the worse your current level of communication, the more drops you insert).
4. Cork the bottle by placing it on a protected surface (a saucer, a box, anything you don't mind ruining).
5. Light the pink candle and wait for the wax to melt a little.
6. Being careful not to burn yourself, pour melted wax over the cap to seal your witch bottle.
7. Now your bottle is ready. Keep in mind that Tuesday is auspicious for love and passion spells, so if possible prefer Tuesday to other days to consecrate your love bottle.
8. Keep the bottle with you at all times.

Witch Bottle For Magnetic Appeal

Difficuty
★

Preparation Time
10 minutes

Use
having a magnetic appeal

Ingredients

◇ A medium-sized dark glass bottle with a cork;
◇ Honey;
◇ Strawberry leaves;
◇ Red rose petals;
◇ Rose water;
◇ Selenite;
◇ Red candle for sealing;

Procedure

1. Fill the bottle halfway with honey.
2. Insert rose petals and strawberry leaves. As you do so repeat, "As these leaves and petals stick to honey, the fascinated gaze of others sticks to me. So I want and so it shall be."
3. Add a few drops of roses.
4. Add selenite.
5. Cork the bottle by placing it on a protected surface (a saucer, a box, anything you don't mind ruining).
6. Light the red candle and wait for the wax to melt a little.
7. Being careful not to burn yourself, pour melted wax over the cap to seal your witch bottle.
8. Now your bottle is ready. Keep in mind that Tuesday is auspicious for love and passion spells, so if possible prefer Tuesday to other days to consecrate your love bottle.
9. Keep the bottle with you at all times.

Witch Bottle to Promote Coexistence

Difficuty
★

Preparation Time
10 minutes

Use
foster coexistence (or improve it)

Ingredients

◇ A medium-sized dark glass bottle with a cork;
◇ Nettles;
◇ Oak leaf;
◇ Coarse salt;
◇ Selenite;
◇ Brown candle for sealing.

Procedure

1. Fill the bottle halfway with rock salt.
2. Insert oak leaf.
3. Insert nettles (possibly using gloves).
4. Add selenite.
5. Cork the bottle by placing it on a protected surface (a saucer, a box, anything you don't mind ruining).
6. Light the brown candle and wait for the wax to melt a little.
7. Being careful not to burn yourself, pour melted wax over the cap to seal your witch bottle.
8. Now your bottle is ready. Keep in mind that Tuesday is auspicious for love and passion spells, so if possible prefer Tuesday to other days to consecrate your love bottle.
9. Keep the bottle with you at all times or in the house you would like to live in with your partner.

Witch Bottle To Promote Marriage

Difficuty
★★★★

Preparation Time
several days to several weeks

Use
Propitiating marriage

Ingredients

◇ A medium-sized dark glass bottle with a cork;
◇ Vase;
◇ Land of a place you keep happy memories of with your partner;
◇ Plant with white flowers of your choice;
◇ Pen
◇ Couple photos;
◇ Pink candle for sealing.

Procedure

1. Recruit from the plant all the flowers that have already bloomed and also the buds.
2. Repot the plant in the loaded soil.
3. Put the plant in the room where you spend the most time as a couple (ex: bedroom).
4. When the first flower has bloomed, sever it.
5. Take the bottle and fill it with half-loaded soil.
6. Insert the flower into the bottle.
7. On the back of the photograph write your intention. For example, "When the next flower blooms, our union in marriage will come true."
8. Roll up the photograph and insert it into the bottle.
9. Cover it with the loaded soil.
10. Cork the bottle by placing it on a protected surface (a saucer, a box, anything you don't mind ruining).
11. Light the pink candle and wait for the wax to melt a little.
12. Being careful not to burn yourself, pour melted wax over the cap to seal your witch bottle.
13. Now your bottle is ready. Keep in mind that Tuesday is auspicious for love and passion spells, so if possible prefer Tuesday to other days to consecrate your love bottle.
14. Keep the bottle hidden under your bed or in a safe place.

Witch Bottle to Make You Say "I Love You"

Difficuty ★★

Preparation Time 10 minutes

Use to propitiate outpourings of love

Ingredients

◇ A medium-sized dark glass bottle with a cork;
◇ Sea salt;
◇ Rose quartz chips;
◇ Three moonstones;
◇ Pen and paper;
◇ Red candle for sealing.

Procedure

1. Fill the bottle halfway with sea salt.
2. Insert rose quartz chips;
3. Insert the three moonstones, one at a time.
4. On the slip of paper write, "I love you, (your name)!" As you do this, imagine your partner's voice as he or she says it to you.
5. Fill the bottle with sea salt to cover all the ingredients.
6. Cork the bottle by placing it on a protected surface (a saucer, a box, anything you don't mind ruining).
7. Light the red candle and wait for the wax to melt a little.
8. Being careful not to burn yourself, pour melted wax over the cap to seal your witch bottle.
9. Now your bottle is ready. Keep in mind that Tuesday is auspicious for love and passion spells, so if possible prefer Tuesday to other days to consecrate your love bottle.
10. Keep the bottle with you at all times.

Witch Bottle To Strengthen Your Feelings

Difficuty

*

Preparation Time

10 minutes

Use

Strengthen your feelings toward the other person

Ingredients

◇ A medium-sized dark glass bottle with a cork;
◇ Lemon and orange peel;
◇ Rosemary;
◇ Couple photos;
◇ Chili pepper;
◇ Lavender essential oil;
◇ Rose thorns;
◇ Red candle for sealing;

Procedure

1. Insert orange and lemon peels into the bottle.
2. Insert your photo taken at a very happy moment into the bottle.
3. Insert the rosemary sprig and dried chili pepper into the bottle.
4. Insert three rose thorns.
5. Add three drops of lavender essential oil.
6. Cork the bottle and place it on a protected surface (a saucer, a box, anything you don't mind ruining).
7. Light the pink candle and wait for the wax to melt a little. In the meantime you can close your eyes again and think hard about the rapprochement between you and your partner. Being careful not to burn yourself pour the melted wax over the cap to seal your witch bottle.
8. Now your bottle is ready. Keep in mind that Tuesday is auspicious for love and passion spells, so if possible prefer Tuesday to other days to consecrate your love bottle.
9. Hide the bottle away from the view of others and, most importantly, in a place where it will not be touched or moved by anyone.

Witch Bottle for Clarity in the Sentimental Field

Difficuty
★★

Preparation Time
10 minutes

Use
mental clarity for feelings

Ingredients

◇ A medium-sized dark glass bottle with a cork;
◇ Rosemary sprig;
◇ Raspberry leaves;
◇ Sandalwood;
◇ Wild bergamot essential oil;
◇ Blue candle for sealing.

Procedure

1. Insert sandalwood into the bottle.
2. Insert the raspberry leaves and add the rosemary sprig.
3. Pour in five drops of wild bergamot essential oil.
4. Cork the bottle and place it on a protected surface (a saucer, a box, anything you don't mind ruining).
5. Light the blue candle and wait for the wax to melt a little. In the meantime you can close your eyes again and think hard about the rapprochement between you and your partner. Being careful not to burn yourself pour the melted wax over the cap to seal your witch bottle.
6. Now your bottle is ready. Keep in mind that Tuesday is auspicious for love and passion spells, so if possible prefer Tuesday to other days to consecrate your love bottle.
7. Hide the bottle under your pillow until you feel you have achieved the desired clarity.

Witch's Bottle For A United Family

Difficuty
*

Preparation Time
10 minutes

Use
Keeping relationships with your family together

Ingredients

◊ A medium-sized dark glass bottle with a cork;
◊ Chrysanthemum petals;
◊ Jasmine petals;
◊ Lavender sprig;
◊ Basil leaves;
◊ Cinnamon stick;
◊ Rose quartz chips;
◊ Rose water;
◊ Family photos;
◊ White candle for sealing;

Procedure

1. Write the name of each family member next to his or her head (including animals) on the photograph.
2. Roll up the photograph, then stick it in the bottle.
3. Enter all flowers and herbs.
4. Add two chips of rose quartz for each family member.
5. Insert the cinnamon stick.
6. Pour a drop of rosewater for each family member.
7. Cork the bottle and place it on a protected surface (a saucer, a box, anything you don't mind ruining).
8. Light the white candle and wait for the wax to melt a little. In the meantime you can close your eyes again and think hard about the rapprochement between you and your partner. Being careful not to burn yourself pour the melted wax over the cap to seal your witch bottle.
9. Now your bottle is ready. Keep in mind that Tuesday is auspicious for love and passion spells, so if possible prefer Tuesday to other days to consecrate your love bottle.
10. Hide the bottle at home, away from the sight of your family members.

Witch Bottle To Mitigate Jealousy

Difficuty
★

Preparation Time
10 minutes

Use
Mitigating jealousy

Ingredients

◇ A medium-sized dark glass bottle with a cork;
◇ Chamomile;
◇ Hyaline quartz;
◇ Sage;
◇ Lavender essential oil;
◇ Sunshine water;
◇ White candle for sealing.

Procedure

1. Insert chamomile flowers.
2. Insert sage.
3. Add hyaline quartz.
4. Pour in eight drops of lavender essential oil.
5. Fill the bottle with sun water.
6. Cork the bottle and place it on a protected surface (a saucer, a box, anything you don't mind ruining).
7. Light the white candle and wait for the wax to melt a little. In the meantime you can close your eyes again and think hard about the rapprochement between you and your partner. Being careful not to burn yourself pour the melted wax over the cap to seal your witch bottle.
8. Now your bottle is ready. Keep in mind that Tuesday is auspicious for love and passion spells, so if possible prefer Tuesday to other days to consecrate your love bottle.
9. Hide the bottle at home, away from the view of your partner or guests.

Witch Bottle To Rekindle Passion

Difficuty
★

Preparation Time
10 minutes

Use
rekindle the fire of passion after years of relationship

Ingredients

◇ A medium-sized dark glass bottle with a cork;
◇ Licorice stick;
◇ Vanilla stick;
◇ Olive leaves;
◇ Violet;
◇ Red wine;
◇ Patchouli essential oil;
◇ Red candle for sealing.

Procedure

1. Insert one licorice stick and one vanilla stick into the bottle.
2. Insert the olive leaves.
3. Insert violets.
4. Add a few drops of patchouli essential oil.
5. Pour in the red wine until the bottle is almost full.
6. Cork the bottle by placing it on a protected surface (a saucer, a box, anything you don't mind ruining).
7. Light the red candle and wait for the wax to melt a little.
8. Being careful not to burn yourself, pour melted wax over the cap to seal your witch bottle.
9. Now your bottle is ready. Keep in mind that Tuesday is auspicious for love and passion spells, so if possible prefer Tuesday to other days to consecrate your love bottle.
10. Hide the bottle under the mattress.

- CHAPTER 6 -

JAR SPELL RECIPES TO ATTRACT WEALTH

Introduction To Bottles For Attracting Wealth And Financial Prosperity

Bottles for attracting abundance have different purposes and varying degrees of intensity. They can be used to attract a small amount of money for an unexpected expenditure, to protect one's already accumulated wealth from theft or debt, to propitiate long-term financial abundance, and more. Several recipes can be prepared according to the purpose. In this chapter we will see how to create Witch bottles to attract wealth in all its forms. Word of advice: if you are a novice, try your hand at the less challenging recipes first. Find the difficulty rating at the beginning of each recipe.

Witch Bottle To Attract Small Amounts Of Money

Difficuty
★★

Preparation Time
10 minutes

Use
Attracting small amounts of money

Ingredients

◇ A medium-sized dark glass bottle with a cork;
◇ 6 coins of your choice as long as the currency you need;
◇ Green ribbon or thread;
◇ 6 dried jasmine flowers;
◇ 6 dried chamomile flowers;
◇ Sheet of paper;
◇ Pen;
◇ Green candle for sealing.

Procedure

1. Insert the 6 jasmine flowers into the bottle;
2. Insert the 6 chamomile flowers into the bottle;
3. Insert coins into the bottle, one at a time, and for each coin focus on the sound it makes when it falls to the bottom.
4. Write on the slip of paper the amount of money you wish to receive, then roll it up as if to form a small parchment.
5. Before you throw the parchment in the bottle, take a few minutes to think hard about the amount of money you intend to receive and how you would feel if you already got it;
6. Insert the green ribbon into the bottle;
7. Cork the bottle and place it on a protected surface (a saucer, a box, anything you don't mind ruining).
8. Light the green candle and wait for the wax to melt a little.
9. Being careful not to burn yourself, pour melted wax over the cap to seal your witch bottle.
10. Now your bottle is ready. Keep in mind that the auspicious day for abundance spells is Sunday, so if possible prefer Sunday to other days to consecrate your bottle of abundance.
11. Hide the bottle away from the view of others and, most importantly, in a place where it will not be touched or moved by anyone. Prefer a place where you usually keep your money, such as a safe, box, etc.

Witch Bottle To Safeguard One's Wealth

Difficuty
★ ★ ★

Preparation Time
15 minutes

Use
Attracting passionate love

Ingredients

◊ A medium-sized dark glass bottle with a cork;
◊ Organic honey;
◊ Dried white and rose petals;
◊ Paper sheet;
◊ Pen;
◊ Rose quartz (rough is best);
◊ Pink Himalayan salt;
◊ Pink candle for sealing.

Procedure

1. Begin the ritual with ten minutes of meditation. Think intensely about your ideal partner, the sensations it causes you, and imagine how you would feel if you were already in the company of your dream partner.
2. Place three dried white (or rose) rose petals in the bottle, careful not to break them.
3. Insert a few pinches of pink Himalayan salt into the bottle.
4. Place rose quartz in the bottle (rough is best, but you can also use a tumbled stone as long as it has been purified beforehand).
5. Take a piece of paper and write in one sentence the most important aspect of a lasting relationship to you.
6. Roll the leaflet up like a small parchment, dip it generously in organic honey, and then insert it into the bottle.
7. Cork the bottle and place it on a protected surface (a saucer, a box, anything you don't mind ruining).
8. Light the pink candle and wait for the wax to melt a little. In the meantime you can close your eyes again and think hard about your intentions.
9. Being careful not to burn yourself, pour melted wax over the cap to seal your witch bottle.
10. Now your bottle is ready. Remember that Tuesday is auspicious for love and passion spells, so if possible prefer Tuesday to other days to consecrate your love bottle.
11. Hide the bottle away from the view of others and, most importantly, in a place where it will not be touched or moved by anyone.

THE JAR SPELLS

Witch Bottle To Attract Large Sums Of Money

Difficuty ★★★★

Preparation Time 10 minutes

Use Attracting large sums of money

Warning: this spell may fall under Black Magic, as you are forcing the will of another individual. Make sure that the person you want to bring back still has positive feelings for you. Otherwise, the attraction you would cause in the other person would only be fictitious and could be counterproductive.

Ingredients

- A large dark glass bottle with a cork;
- Coarse salt;
- Oleolite of St. John's Wort;
- 6 dried jasmine flowers;
- 6 dried chamomile flowers;
- Cinnamon stick;
- Large denomination banknote in the current currency;
- Green thread;
- Sheet of paper;
- Pen;
- Green candle for sealing;

1. Insert the 6 jasmine flowers into the bottle;
2. Insert the 6 chamomile flowers into the bottle;
3. Roll the large denomination bill onto itself and secure it with green ribbon through a knot (not a bow-it must be a tight knot that is impossible to untie).
4. Insert the rolled bill into the bottle.
5. Write on the slip the amount of money you wish to receive, then roll it up as if to form a small parchment.
6. Before you throw the parchment in the bottle, take a few minutes to think hard about the amount of money you intend to receive and how you would feel if you already got it.
7. Bury the ingredients in the bottle with coarse salt.
8. Pour 6 drops of St. John's Wort oleolite into the bottle, over the coarse salt poured earlier.
9. Insert the cinnamon stick into the bottle by making it stand upright. To accomplish this you can sink it a few inches into the coarse salt.
10. Cork the bottle and place it on a protected surface (a saucer, a box, anything you don't mind ruining).
11. Light the green candle and wait for the wax to melt a little.
12. Being careful not to burn yourself, pour melted wax over the cap to seal your witch bottle.
13. Now your bottle is ready. Keep in mind that the auspicious day for abundance spells is Sunday, so if possible prefer Sunday to other days to consecrate your bottle of abundance.
14. Hide the bottle away from the sight of others and, most importantly, in a place where it will not be touched or moved by anyone. Prefer a place where you usually keep your money, such as a safe, box, etc.

Witch Bottle To Attract Prosperity

Difficuty
★★★

Preparation Time
5 minutes

Use
Attracting prosperity

Ingredients

◇ A large dark glass bottle with a cork;
◇ Dried basil;
◇ Juniper berries;
◇ Jade chips;
◇ Green thread;
◇ Green candle for sealing.

Procedure

1. Insert the dried basil leaves into the bottle;
2. Place in the bottle of juniper, one at a time;
3. Insert jade chips into the bottle;
4. Insert the green wire into the bottle;
5. Cork the bottle and place it on a protected surface (a saucer, a box, anything you don't mind ruining).
6. Light the green candle and wait for the wax to melt a little.
7. Being careful not to burn yourself, pour melted wax over the cap to seal your witch bottle.
8. Now your bottle is ready. Keep in mind that the auspicious day for abundance spells is Sunday, so if possible prefer Sunday to other days to consecrate your bottle of abundance.
9. Hide the bottle away from the view of others and, most importantly, in a place where it will not be touched or moved by anyone.

Witch Bottle To Attract Financial Well-Being

Difficuty
★ ★ ★

Preparation Time
5 minutes

Use
Attracting financial wealth

Ingredients

◇ A large dark glass bottle with a cork;
◇ 5 one-euro coins;
◇ 5 coins of 50 cents;
◇ 5 coins one cent;
◇ 5 sesame seeds;
◇ 5 cinnamon sticks;
◇ 5 green peppercorns;
◇ 5 pecans;
◇ Green candle for sealing.

Procedure

1. Insert euro coins into the bottle, one at a time, and for each coin focus on the sound it makes when it falls to the bottom.
2. Insert the 50-cent coins into the bottle, one at a time, and for each coin focus on the sound it makes when it falls to the bottom.
3. Insert penny coins into the bottle, one at a time, and for each coin focus on the sound it makes when it falls to the bottom.
4. Add the 5 sesame seeds, 5 green peppercorns, and 5 pecans;
5. Insert the 5 cinnamon sticks into the bottle;
6. Cork the bottle and place it on a protected surface (a saucer, a box, anything you don't mind ruining).
7. Light the green candle and wait for the wax to melt a little.
8. Being careful not to burn yourself, pour melted wax over the cap to seal your witch bottle.
9. Now your bottle is ready. Keep in mind that the auspicious day for abundance spells is Sunday, so if possible prefer Sunday to other days to consecrate your bottle of abundance.
10. Hide the bottle away from the view of others and, most importantly, in a place where it will not be touched or moved by anyone.

Witch Bottle to Attract a Promotion at Work

Difficuty
★

Preparation Time
10 minutes

Use
Attracting a promotion

Ingredients

◊ A medium-sized dark glass bottle with a cork;
◊ Ginger;
◊ Green thread;
◊ Pen and paper;
◊ Bergamot essential oil;
◊ Green candle for sealing.

Procedure

1. Insert the ginger into the bottle.
2. Insert the green wire into the bottle.
3. On a piece of paper write down what is the net salary you would like in view of your promotion, then place it in the bottle.
4. Add 5 drops of bergamot essential oil. As you do this, visualize your boss shaking your hand congratulating you on your promotion.
5. Cork the bottle and place it on a protected surface (a saucer, a box, anything you don't mind ruining).
6. Light the green candle and wait for the wax to melt a little.
7. Being careful not to burn yourself, pour melted wax over the cap to seal your witch bottle.
8. Now your bottle is ready. Keep in mind that the auspicious day for abundance spells is Sunday, so if possible prefer Sunday to other days to consecrate your bottle of abundance.
9. Hide the bottle away from the view of others and, most importantly, in a place where it will not be touched or moved by anyone.

Witch Bottle To Make a Business Flourish Again

Difficuty
★ ★

Preparation Time
20 minutes

Use
Making a business in crisis flourish again

Ingredients

◇ A medium-sized dark glass bottle with a cork;
◇ Ginger;
◇ Olive branch;
◇ Oak leaf;
◇ Mandrake root;
◇ Sandalwood;
◇ Bergamot essential oil;
◇ Green candle for sealing.

Procedure

1. Light the sandalwood and let it burn in a container so that the ashes are collected. Once the ashes have cooled put them in the bottle.
2. Place ginger and mandrake root in the bottle.
3. Insert the oak leaf and olive branch into the bottle.
4. Add 5 drops of bergamot essential oil. As you do this, visualize your business in the midst of its success.
5. Cork the bottle and place it on a protected surface (a saucer, a box, anything you don't mind ruining).
6. Light the green candle and wait for the wax to melt a little.
7. Being careful not to burn yourself, pour melted wax over the cap to seal your witch bottle.
8. Now your bottle is ready. Keep in mind that the auspicious day for abundance spells is Sunday, so if possible prefer Sunday to other days to consecrate your bottle of abundance.
9. Hide the bottle inside your business, preferably near the front door or cash register. Make sure it is not visible or reachable by anyone.

Witch Bottle for a Successful Idea

Difficuty
*

Preparation Time
10 minutes

Use
Having a successful idea

Ingredients

◇ A small, dark glass bottle with a cork;
◇ Cinnamon stick;
◇ Bay leaves;
◇ Beech leaf;
◇ Amber;
◇ Carnelian chips;
◇ Moon water;
◇ Orange candle for sealing.

Procedure

1. Insert bay leaves and beech leaf into the bottle;
2. Add carnelian chips.
3. Add the amber stone.
4. Insert the cinnamon stick into the bottle;
5. Add 5 drops of moonshine water.
6. Cork the bottle and place it on a protected surface (a saucer, a box, anything you don't mind ruining).
7. Light the green candle and wait for the wax to melt a little.
8. Being careful not to burn yourself, pour melted wax over the cap to seal your witch bottle.
9. Now your bottle is ready. Keep in mind that the auspicious day for abundance spells is Sunday, so if possible prefer Sunday to other days to consecrate your bottle of abundance.
10. Hide the bottle under your pillow so that the idea of success reaches you in your sleep.

Witch's Bottle To Make The Right Decision

Difficuty
✳

Preparation Time
10 minutes

Use
making the right decision

Ingredients

◇ A small, dark glass bottle with a cork;
◇ Amber;
◇ Narcissus;
◇ Iolite;
◇ Pine needles;
◇ Sunshine water;
◇ Orange candle for sealing.

Procedure

1. Insert the pine needles into the bottle, one at a time.
2. Add the iolite stone.
3. Add the amber stone.
4. Insert some freshly cut daffodil flowers into the bottle.
5. Add 5 drops of sun water.
6. Cork the bottle and place it on a protected surface (a saucer, a box, anything you don't mind ruining).
7. Light the orange candle and wait for the wax to melt a little.
8. Being careful not to burn yourself, pour melted wax over the cap to seal your witch bottle.
9. Now your bottle is ready. Keep in mind that the auspicious day for abundance spells is Sunday, so if possible prefer Sunday to other days to consecrate your bottle of abundance.
10. Hide the bottle under your pillow so that the right choice will reveal itself to you in your sleep.

Witch Bottle For Being Influential

Difficuty ★★

Preparation Time 20 minutes

Use being influential and charismatic

Ingredients

◊ A medium-sized dark glass bottle with a cork;
◊ Sodalite chips;
◊ Wild bergamot essential oil;
◊ Thyme;
◊ Acorns;
◊ Cluster of white sage;
◊ Golden candle for sealing.

Procedure

1. Light the bunch of white sage and let it burn in a container so that the ashes are collected. Once the ashes have cooled put them in the bottle.
2. Insert sodalite chips into the bottle.
3. Insert the thyme into the bottle.
4. Add 5 acorns.
5. Add 5 drops of wild bergamot essential oil.
6. Cork the bottle and place it on a protected surface (a saucer, a box, anything you don't mind ruining).
7. Light the green candle and wait for the wax to melt a little.
8. Being careful not to burn yourself, pour melted wax over the cap to seal your witch bottle.
9. Now your bottle is ready. Keep in mind that the auspicious day for abundance spells is Sunday, so if possible prefer Sunday to other days to consecrate your bottle of abundance.
10. Keep the bottle with you at all times, in a pocket or purse.

Witch Bottle To Banish Procrastination

Difficuty
★ ★ ★

Preparation Time
10 minutes

Use
stop procrastinating and become productive again

Ingredients

◇ A medium-sized dark glass bottle with a cork;
◇ Sea salt;
◇ Orange blossom;
◇ Beech leaf;
◇ Pins;
◇ Rhodonite;
◇ Wild bergamot essential oil;
◇ Orange candle for sealing.

Procedure

1. Fill the bottle halfway with sea salt.
2. Insert the rhodonite stone into the bottle.
3. Insert orange blossom and beech leaf into the bottle.
4. Add 5 pins, one at a time.
5. Add 5 drops of wild bergamot essential oil.
6. Cork the bottle and place it on a protected surface (a saucer, a box, anything you don't mind ruining).
7. Light the orange candle and wait for the wax to melt a little.
8. Being careful not to burn yourself, pour melted wax over the cap to seal your witch bottle.
9. Now your bottle is ready. Keep in mind that the auspicious day for abundance spells is Sunday, so if possible prefer Sunday to other days to consecrate your bottle of abundance.
10. Keep the bottle in your workspace for 21 days, then bury it.

Bottle Of The Millionaire's Witch

Difficuty
★ ★ ★

Preparation Time
10 minutes

Use
propitiating success through a mentor

Ingredients

◇ A medium-sized dark glass bottle with a cork;
◇ Coarse salt;
◇ Corn syrup;
◇ A picture of a millionaire you would like to be inspired by;
◇ A picture of you;
◇ Green ribbon;
◇ Golden candle for sealing.

Procedure

1. Take the photo of the millionaire character whose path to success you would like to trace. Spread a thick layer of corn syrup on the front, then take your photo and paste it face down on the front of the other photograph, in a kind of sandwich.
2. Roll the two photos on themselves and fasten them with green ribbon, then place them in the bottle.
3. Cover with coarse salt until full.
4. Cork the bottle and place it on a protected surface (a saucer, a box, anything you don't mind ruining).
5. Light the gold candle and wait for the wax to melt a little.
6. Being careful not to burn yourself, pour melted wax over the cap to seal your witch bottle.
7. Now your bottle is ready. Keep in mind that the auspicious day for abundance spells is Sunday, so if possible prefer Sunday to other days to consecrate your bottle of abundance.
8. Keep the bottle in your work space away from prying eyes.

Witch Bottle To Ward Off Debt

Difficuty *

Preparation Time 10 minutes

Use to have no more debt

Ingredients

◇ A small, dark glass bottle with a cork;
◇ Papers, unpaid bills, eviction letters, etc. (anything that makes you feel like a failure and that you feel you can't fix);
◇ Biodegradable gold glitter;
◇ White candle for sealing.

Procedure

1. Put all the papers in a suitable container to hold the ashes and set them on fire with a match.
2. Once the ashes have cooled put them in the bottle.
3. Add a sprinkling of glitter.
4. Shake the bottle so that the ash mixes evenly with the glitter.
5. Cork the bottle and place it on a protected surface (a saucer, a box, anything you don't mind ruining).
6. Light the white candle and wait for the wax to melt a little.
7. Being careful not to burn yourself, pour melted wax over the cap to seal your witch bottle.
8. Now your bottle is ready. Keep in mind that the auspicious day for abundance spells is Sunday, so if possible prefer Sunday to other days to consecrate your bottle of abundance.
9. Keep the bottle in your work space away from prying eyes.

Witch Bottle To Get A Mortgage Or Loan

Difficuty
★

Preparation Time
10 minutes

Use
obtaining a mortgage or loan

Ingredients

◊ A small, dark glass bottle with a cork;
◊ Coarse salt;
◊ Pen and paper;
◊ Cinnamon powder;
◊ Green candle for sealing.

Procedure

1. Fill the bottle halfway with rock salt.
2. On a piece of paper write the amount you wish to borrow, fold it back on itself, and put it in the bottle.
3. Cover with sea salt until the bottle is full.
4. Add a sprinkling of cinnamon on top.
5. Cork the bottle and place it on a protected surface (a saucer, a box, anything you don't mind ruining).
6. Light the green candle and wait for the wax to melt a little.
7. Being careful not to burn yourself, pour melted wax over the cap to seal your witch bottle.
8. Now your bottle is ready. Keep in mind that the auspicious day for abundance spells is Sunday, so if possible prefer Sunday to other days to consecrate your bottle of abundance.
9. Keep the bottle in your safe or in the place where you usually keep your money.

Witch's Bottle For Living In Abundance

Difficuty
★ ★

Preparation Time
10 minutes

Use
living in abundance

Ingredients

◇ A medium-sized dark glass bottle with a cork;
◇ Pimenta dioica;
◇ Basil leaves;
◇ Malachite;
◇ Sea salt;
◇ Moon eclipse water;
◇ Green candle for sealing.

Procedure

1. Enter pimenta dioica.
2. Add the basil leaves.
3. Add malachite.
4. Cover with sea salt until the bottle is full.
5. Add 5 drops of eclipse moon water.
6. Cork the bottle and place it on a protected surface (a saucer, a box, anything you don't mind ruining).
7. Light the green candle and wait for the wax to melt a little.
8. Being careful not to burn yourself, pour melted wax over the cap to seal your witch bottle.
9. Now your bottle is ready. Keep in mind that the auspicious day for abundance spells is Sunday, so if possible prefer Sunday to other days to consecrate your bottle of abundance.
10. Keep the bottle with you or in your home.

Witch Bottle For The Event

Difficuty
★★

Preparation Time
10 minutes

Use
Manifest with ease

Ingredients

- A medium-sized dark glass bottle with a cork;
- Bay leaves;
- Sea salt;
- Pyrite chips;
- Carnelian chips;
- Pen and paper;
- Gold candle for sealing.

Procedure

1. Insert bay leaves into the bottle;
2. Place the pyrite and carnelian chips previously mixed together in the bottle;
3. On a piece of paper write down in which field you would like to receive abundance, then fold it back on itself and insert it into the bottle.
4. Cover with sea salt until the bottle is full.
5. Cork the bottle and place it on a protected surface (a saucer, a box, anything you don't mind ruining).
6. Light the gold candle and wait for the wax to melt a little.
7. Being careful not to burn yourself, pour melted wax over the cap to seal your witch bottle.
8. Now your bottle is ready. Keep in mind that the auspicious day for abundance spells is Sunday, so if possible prefer Sunday to other days to consecrate your bottle of abundance.
9. Think hard about the object of your desire, then bury the bottle.

Witch Bottle for the Full Wallet

Difficuty ★ ★ ★

Preparation Time 30 minutes

Use always have a full wallet

Ingredients

- A medium-sized dark glass bottle with a cork;
- Peppermint;
- Tiger eye;
- Cascara sagrada;
- Blackberry juice;
- Moon water;
- Green candle for sealing.

Procedure

1. Insert peppermint into the bottle;
2. Insert the tiger's eye into the bottle;
3. Add cascara sagrada;
4. Take two fistfuls of blackberries and boil them in a saucepan with a few drops of moon water until you get a juice. Wait for the mixture to cool, then pass it through a strainer. Finally place the juice in the bottle.
5. Cork the bottle and place it on a protected surface (a saucer, a box, anything you don't mind ruining).
6. Light the green candle and wait for the wax to melt a little.
7. Being careful not to burn yourself, pour melted wax over the cap to seal your witch bottle.
8. Now your bottle is ready. Keep in mind that the auspicious day for abundance spells is Sunday, so if possible prefer Sunday to other days to consecrate your bottle of abundance.
9. Keep the bottle in a drawer, where you will also store your wallet each night.

Witch's Bottle To Recover A Lost Sum

Difficuty
★ ★

Preparation Time
10 minutes

Use
Attracting a promotion

Ingredients

◇ A medium-sized dark glass bottle with a cork;
◇ Green ribbon or thread;
◇ 6 dried jasmine flowers;
◇ 6 dried chamomile flowers;
◇ Holly;
◇ Nutmeg;
◇ Peppermint essential oil;
◇ Green candle for sealing.

Procedure

1. Place 6 jasmine flowers and 6 chamomile flowers in the bottle.
2. Insert holly.
3. Add nutmeg.
4. Insert the green ribbon.
5. Pour in a few drops of peppermint essential oil.
6. Cork the bottle and place it on a protected surface (a saucer, a box, anything you don't mind ruining).
7. Light the green candle and wait for the wax to melt a little.
8. Being careful not to burn yourself, pour melted wax over the cap to seal your witch bottle.
9. Now your bottle is ready. Keep in mind that the auspicious day for abundance spells is Sunday, so if possible prefer Sunday to other days to consecrate your bottle of abundance.
10. Keep the bottle in a drawer or safe until you reottienize the figure perdura.

Witch Bottle to Counter Wastefulness

Difficuty
*

Preparation Time
10 minutes

Use
to counter waste of money.

Ingredients

- A medium-sized dark glass bottle with a cork;
- Coarse salt;
- Verbena;
- Cascara sagrada;
- Rose quartz;
- Padlock;
- Green candle for sealing.

Procedure

1. Fill the bottle halfway with rock salt.
2. Add verbena.
3. Add cascara sagrada.
4. Insert rose quartz.
5. Insert the padlock into the bottle (it must be locked and keyless).
6. Cover with coarse salt until the bottle is full.
7. Cork the bottle and place it on a protected surface (a saucer, a box, anything you don't mind ruining).
8. Light the green candle and wait for the wax to melt a little.
9. Being careful not to burn yourself, pour melted wax over the cap to seal your witch bottle.
10. Now your bottle is ready. Keep in mind that the auspicious day for abundance spells is Sunday, so if possible prefer Sunday to other days to consecrate your bottle of abundance.
11. Keep the bottle in a drawer, where you will also store your wallet each night.

Witch Bottle To Counteract Avarice

Difficuty
★

Preparation Time
10 minutes

Use
to counter avarice and promote generosity

Ingredients

◇ A medium-sized dark glass bottle with a cork;
◇ Coarse salt;
◇ Lime tree;
◇ Jasmine flowers;
◇ Mallow extract;
◇ Padlock;
◇ Yellow candle for sealing.

Procedure

1. Fill the bottle halfway with rock salt.
2. Add the linden leaf.
3. Add jasmine flowers.
4. Insert the padlock into the bottle (it must be open) and the key to it.
5. Cover with mallow extract.
6. Cork the bottle and place it on a protected surface (a saucer, a box, anything you don't mind ruining).
7. Light the yellow candle and wait for the wax to melt a little.
8. Being careful not to burn yourself, pour melted wax over the cap to seal your witch bottle.
9. Now your bottle is ready. Keep in mind that the auspicious day for abundance spells is Sunday, so if possible prefer Sunday to other days to consecrate your bottle of abundance.
10. Keep the bottle in a drawer, where you will also store your wallet each night.

- CHAPTER 7 -

JAR SPELL RECIPES TO ATTRACT GOOD LUCK

Bottles for attracting abundance have different purposes and varying degrees of intensity. They can be used to attract a small amount of money for an unexpected expenditure, to protect one's already accumulated wealth from theft or debt, to propitiate long-term financial abundance, and more. There are several recipes that can be prepared according to the purpose. In this chapter we will see how to create Witch bottles to attract wealth in all its forms. A word of advice: if you are a beginner, try your hand at the less challenging recipes first. Find the difficulty rating at the beginning of each recipe.

Witch Bottle To Attract Luck In Love

Difficuty
★ ★

Preparation Time
10 minutes

Use
Attracting luck in love

Ingredients

◇ A medium-sized dark glass bottle with a cork;
◇ Red rose petals;
◇ Four-leaf clover;
◇ Poppy petals;
◇ Rose quartz;
◇ Rose water;
◇ Green candle for sealing.

Procedure

1. Insert the red rose petals.
2. Add poppy petals.
3. Add rose quartz.
4. Add the four-leaf clover.
5. Fill the bottle with rosewater.
6. Cork the bottle and place it on a protected surface (a saucer, a box, anything you don't mind ruining).
7. Light the green candle and wait for the wax to melt a little.
8. Being careful not to burn yourself, pour melted wax over the cap to seal your witch bottle.
9. Now your bottle is ready. Keep in mind that the auspicious day for fortune spells is Thursday, so if possible prefer Thursday to other days to consecrate your fortune bottle.
10. He buries the bottle.

Witch Bottle To Get Your Dream Job

Difficuty ★

Preparation Time 10 minutes

Use Attracting good fortune in business

Ingredients

◊ A medium-sized dark glass bottle with a cork;
◊ Pen and paper;
◊ Your resume;
◊ Four-leaf clover;
◊ Honey;
◊ Ginger;
◊ Green candle for sealing.

Procedure

1. On a piece of paper, write down what your dream job or position is that you are applying for
2. Roll it up and put it in the bottle.
3. Add a copy of your resume to the bottle.
4. Add a tablespoon of honey and the ginger.
5. Add the four-leaf clover.
6. Cork the bottle and place it on a protected surface (a saucer, a box, anything you don't mind ruining).
7. Light the green candle and wait for the wax to melt a little.
8. Being careful not to burn yourself, pour melted wax over the cap to seal your witch bottle.
9. Now your bottle is ready. Keep in mind that the auspicious day for fortune spells is Thursday, so if possible prefer Thursday to other days to consecrate your fortune bottle.
10. He buries the bottle.

Witch Bottle To Attract Luck In The Lottery

Difficuty
★

Preparation Time
10 minutes

Use
Attracting luck to the lottery

Ingredients

◇ A medium-sized dark glass bottle with a cork;
◇ 6 coins of your choice as long as the currency you need;
◇ A four-leaf clover;
◇ Pen and paper;
◇ Green candle for sealing.

Procedure

1. Insert coins into the bottle, one at a time, and for each coin focus on the sound it makes when it falls to the bottom.
2. Write on the slip of paper the amount of money you wish to receive, then roll it up as if to form a small parchment.
3. Before you throw the parchment in the bottle, take a few minutes to think hard about the amount of money you intend to receive and how you would feel if you already got it;
4. Insert the four-leaf clover into the bottle;
5. Cork the bottle and place it on a protected surface (a saucer, a box, anything you don't mind ruining).
6. Light the green candle and wait for the wax to melt a little.
7. Being careful not to burn yourself, pour melted wax over the cap to seal your witch bottle.
8. Now your bottle is ready. Keep in mind that the auspicious day for fortune spells is Thursday, so if possible prefer Thursday to other days to consecrate your fortune bottle.
9. He buries the bottle.

Witch Bottle To Attract Luck In Sports

Difficuty
★

Preparation Time
5 minutes

Use
Attracting luck in sports

Ingredients

◇ A medium-sized dark glass bottle with a cork;
◇ Cinnamon powder;
◇ Subject inherent to the sport played;
◇ Four-leaf clover;
◇ Aloe vera juice;
◇ Green candle for sealing.

Procedure

1. Insert cinnamon powder;
2. Add the object inherent to your sport (ex: tennis-a piece of a tennis ball).
3. Add the four-leaf clover.
4. Fill with aloe vera juice.
5. Cork the bottle and place it on a protected surface (a saucer, a box, anything you don't mind ruining).
6. Light the green candle and wait for the wax to melt a little.
7. Being careful not to burn yourself, pour melted wax over the cap to seal your witch bottle.
8. Now your bottle is ready. Keep in mind that the auspicious day for fortune spells is Thursday, so if possible prefer Thursday to other days to consecrate your fortune bottle.
9. He buries the bottle.

Witch's Bottle To Find A Lost Object

Difficuty
★

Preparation Time
10 minutes

Use
Witch's Bottle To Find A Lost Object

Ingredients

◇ A medium-sized dark glass bottle with a cork;
◇ Pen and paper;
◇ Four-leaf clover;
◇ Holly;
◇ Adventurine chips;
◇ Green candle for sealing.

Procedure

1. On a slip of paper, describe the lost item. Roll it up and put it in the bottle.
2. Add aventurine chips to the bottle;
3. Add the four-leaf clover to the bottle;
4. Add holly;
5. Cork the bottle and place it on a protected surface (a saucer, a box, anything you don't mind ruining).
6. Light the green candle and wait for the wax to melt a little.
7. Being careful not to burn yourself, pour melted wax over the cap to seal your witch bottle.
8. Now your bottle is ready. Keep in mind that the auspicious day for fortune spells is Thursday, so if possible prefer Thursday to other days to consecrate your fortune bottle.
9. He buries the bottle.

Witch Bottle To Banish Bad Luck

Difficuty
*

Preparation Time
10 minutes

Use
banishing bad luck

Ingredients

◇ A medium-sized dark glass bottle with a cork;
◇ Lime tree;
◇ Three four-leaf clovers;
◇ A picture of you;
◇ Amber;
◇ Jasmine essential oil;
◇ Green candle for sealing.

Procedure

1. Insert the three four-leaf clovers into the bottle.
2. Add the linden leaf.
3. Add amber.
4. Add your photo folded in on itself.
5. Pour in a few drops of jasmine essential oil.
6. Cork the bottle and place it on a protected surface (a saucer, a box, anything you don't mind ruining).
7. Light the green candle and wait for the wax to melt a little.
8. Being careful not to burn yourself, pour melted wax over the cap to seal your witch bottle.
9. Now your bottle is ready. Keep in mind that the auspicious day for fortune spells is Thursday, so if possible prefer Thursday to other days to consecrate your fortune bottle. Bury the bottle.

Witch Bottle To Be In The Right Place At The Right Time

Difficuty
★

Preparation Time
10 minutes

Use
Being in the right place at the right time.

Ingredients

◇ A medium-sized dark glass bottle with a cork;
◇ Hypericum flowers;
◇ Four-leaf clover;
◇ Honey;
◇ Adventurine chips;
◇ Green candle for sealing.

Procedure

1. Insert the honey into the bottle.
2. Add the four-leaf clover.
3. Add three flowers of St. John's Wort.
4. Add aventurine chips.
5. Cork the bottle and place it on a protected surface (a saucer, a box, anything you don't mind ruining).
6. Light the green candle and wait for the wax to melt a little.
7. Being careful not to burn yourself, pour melted wax over the cap to seal your witch bottle.
8. Now your bottle is ready. Keep in mind that the auspicious day for fortune spells is Thursday, so if possible prefer Thursday to other days to consecrate your fortune bottle. Bury the bottle.

Witch Bottle To Stay Healthy All The Time

Difficuty
★

Preparation Time
10 minutes

Use
good health, ward off disease

Ingredients

- A medium-sized dark glass bottle with a cork;
- Ash leaf;
- Four-leaf clover;
- Mandrake root;
- Nutmeg;
- A picture of you;
- Green candle for sealing.

Procedure

1. Enter the nutmeg.
2. Add the four-leaf clover.
3. Add mandrake root;
4. Add the ash leaf.
5. Add your photo folded in on itself.
6. Cork the bottle and place it on a protected surface (a saucer, a box, anything you don't mind ruining).
7. Light the green candle and wait for the wax to melt a little.
8. Being careful not to burn yourself, pour melted wax over the cap to seal your witch bottle.
9. Now your bottle is ready. Keep in mind that the auspicious day for fortune spells is Thursday, so if possible prefer Thursday to other days to consecrate your fortune bottle. Bury the bottle.

Witch Bottle To Make A Wish Come True

Difficuty
★

Preparation Time
10 minutes

Use
Fulfilling a wish

Ingredients

◊ A medium-sized dark glass bottle with a cork;
◊ Beech leaf;
◊ Blueberry juice;
◊ Four-leaf clover;
◊ Carnelian chips;
◊ Pen and paper;
◊ Green candle for sealing.

Procedure

1. On a piece of paper describe the object of your desires. Roll it up and put it in the bottle.
2. Insert the beech leaf.
3. Add carnelian chips.
4. Add the four-leaf clover.
5. Pour in the blueberry juice until full.
6. Cork the bottle and place it on a protected surface (a saucer, a box, anything you don't mind ruining).
7. Light the green candle and wait for the wax to melt a little.
8. Being careful not to burn yourself, pour melted wax over the cap to seal your witch bottle.
9. Now your bottle is ready. Keep in mind that the auspicious day for fortune spells is Thursday, so if possible prefer Thursday to other days to consecrate your fortune bottle. Bury the bottle.

Witch Bottle To Attract Luck In A Specific Area

Difficuty

★

Preparation Time

10 minutes

Use

Attracting luck in a specific area of your choice

Ingredients

◇ A medium-sized dark glass bottle with a cork;
◇ Four-leaf clover;
◇ Violets;
◇ Carnelian chips;
◇ Pen and paper;
◇ Green candle for sealing.

Procedure

1. On a piece of paper describe the object of your desires. Roll it up and put it in the bottle.
2. Insert violets.
3. Add carnelian chips.
4. Add the four-leaf clover.
5. Cork the bottle and place it on a protected surface (a saucer, a box, anything you don't mind ruining).
6. Light the green candle and wait for the wax to melt a little.
7. Being careful not to burn yourself, pour melted wax over the cap to seal your witch bottle.
8. Now your bottle is ready. Keep in mind that the auspicious day for fortune spells is Thursday, so if possible prefer Thursday to other days to consecrate your fortune bottle. Bury the bottle.

Witch's Bottle For The Sex Of The Unborn Child

Difficuty

★

Preparation Time

10 minutes

Use

influencing the sex of the unborn child

Ingredients

◊ A medium-sized dark glass bottle with a cork;
◊ Four-leaf clover;
◊ Blue or pink ribbon;
◊ Peach blossoms;
◊ Rhodonite;
◊ Green candle for sealing.

Procedure

1. On a piece of paper describe the object of your desires. Roll it up and put it in the bottle.
2. Insert peach blossoms.
3. Add pink or blue ribbon.
4. Add rhodonite.
5. Add the four-leaf clover.
6. Cork the bottle and place it on a protected surface (a saucer, a box, anything you don't mind ruining).
7. Light the green candle and wait for the wax to melt a little.
8. Being careful not to burn yourself, pour melted wax over the cap to seal your witch bottle.
9. Now your bottle is ready. Keep in mind that the auspicious day for fortune spells is Thursday, so if possible prefer Thursday to other days to consecrate your fortune bottle. Bury the bottle

Witch Bottle for Renewal of Labor Contract

Difficuty: *

Preparation Time: 15 minutes

Use: maintaining the workplace

Ingredients

◊ A large dark glass bottle with a cork;
◊ A copy of your employment contract;
◊ Four-leaf clover;
◊ Honey;
◊ Poppy petals;
◊ Green candle for sealing.

Procedure

1. Print a copy of your employment contract. With a pen, change the contract end date (e.g., 2022 2023). Fold it up and put it in the bottle.
2. Enter the four-leaf clover.
3. Add honey.
4. Add poppy petals.
5. Cork the bottle and place it on a protected surface (a saucer, a box, anything you don't mind ruining).
6. Light the green candle and wait for the wax to melt a little.
7. Being careful not to burn yourself, pour melted wax over the cap to seal your witch bottle.
8. Now your bottle is ready. Keep in mind that the auspicious day for fortune spells is Thursday, so if possible prefer Thursday to other days to consecrate your fortune bottle. Bury the bottle.

Witch Bottle To Receive The Perfect Gift

Difficuty
*

Preparation Time
10 minutes

Use
Attracting good fortune in business

Ingredients

◇ A large dark glass bottle with a cork;
◇ Four-leaf clover;
◇ Pen and paper;
◇ Dandelion honey;
◇ Carnelian chips;
◇ Green candle for sealing.

Procedure

1. On a piece of paper describe the object of your desires. Roll it up and put it in the bottle.
2. Add dandelion honey.
3. Add the four-leaf clover.
4. Add carnelian chips.
5. Cork the bottle and place it on a protected surface (a saucer, a box, anything you don't mind ruining).
6. Light the green candle and wait for the wax to melt a little.
7. Being careful not to burn yourself, pour melted wax over the cap to seal your witch bottle.
8. Now your bottle is ready. Keep in mind that the auspicious day for fortune spells is Thursday, so if possible prefer Thursday to other days to consecrate your fortune bottle. Bury the bottle

Witch Bottle To Find The Car Of Your Dreams

Difficuty

★

Preparation Time

10 minutes

Use

finding the car of your dreams

Ingredients

- A large dark glass bottle with a cork;
- Photos of your dream car;
- Four-leaf clover;
- Jasmine;
- Honey;
- Green candle for sealing.

Procedure

1. Insert a picture of your dream car into the bottle.
2. Add honey.
3. Add the four-leaf clover.
4. Add three jasmine flowers.
5. Cork the bottle and place it on a protected surface (a saucer, a box, anything you don't mind ruining).
6. Light the green candle and wait for the wax to melt a little.
7. Being careful not to burn yourself, pour melted wax over the cap to seal your witch bottle.
8. Now your bottle is ready. Keep in mind that the auspicious day for fortune spells is Thursday, so if possible prefer Thursday to other days to consecrate your fortune bottle. Bury the bottle.

Bottle of the Witch to Find Your Dream Home

Difficuty

★

Preparation Time

10 minutes

Use

Attracting your dream home

Ingredients

◊ A large dark glass bottle with a cork;
◊ Photos of your dream home;
◊ Pen and paper;
◊ Four-leaf clover;
◊ Nutmeg;
◊ Honey;
◊ Green candle for sealing.

Procedure

1. Insert a picture of your dream house into the bottle.
2. On a piece of paper, describe your dream house in great detail. Fold it up and insert it into the bottle.
3. Add honey.
4. Add the four-leaf clover.
5. Add nutmeg.
6. Cork the bottle and place it on a protected surface (a saucer, a box, anything you don't mind ruining).
7. Light the green candle and wait for the wax to melt a little.
8. Being careful not to burn yourself, pour melted wax over the cap to seal your witch bottle.
9. Now your bottle is ready. Keep in mind that the auspicious day for fortune spells is Thursday, so if possible prefer Thursday to other days to consecrate your fortune bottle. Bury the bottle.

Witch's Bottle To Always Have Good Luck

Difficuty
★

Preparation Time
10 minutes

Use
persistent luck

Ingredients

◊ A large dark glass bottle with a cork;
◊ Cinnamon powder;
◊ Three four-leaf clovers;
◊ Three clovers;
◊ Yellow rose petals;
◊ Agate;
◊ Green candle for sealing.

Procedure

1. Insert the yellow rose petals into the bottle.
2. Add honey.
3. Add three four-leaf clovers.
4. Add three clovers.
5. Add cinnamon powder.
6. Insert agate.
7. Cork the bottle and place it on a protected surface (a saucer, a box, anything you don't mind ruining).
8. Light the green candle and wait for the wax to melt a little.
9. Being careful not to burn yourself, pour melted wax over the cap to seal your witch bottle.
10. Now your bottle is ready. Keep in mind that the auspicious day for fortune spells is Thursday, so if possible prefer Thursday to other days to consecrate your fortune bottle. Bury the bottle.

Witch's Bottle for a Lucky Meeting

Difficuty
*

Preparation Time
10 minutes

Use
to foster a lucky encounter

Ingredients

◇ A medium-sized dark glass bottle with a cork;
◇ Four-leaf clover;
◇ Violets;
◇ Carnelian chips;
◇ Rose water;
◇ Green candle for sealing.

Procedure

1. Insert the violets into the bottle.
2. Add the four-leaf clover.
3. Add carnelian chips.
4. Fill with rosewater.
5. Cork the bottle and place it on a protected surface (a saucer, a box, anything you don't mind ruining).
6. Light the green candle and wait for the wax to melt a little.
7. Being careful not to burn yourself, pour melted wax over the cap to seal your witch bottle.
8. Now your bottle is ready. Keep in mind that the auspicious day for fortune spells is Thursday, so if possible prefer Thursday to other days to consecrate your fortune bottle. Bury the bottle.

To Always Arrive On Time

Difficuty
*

Preparation Time
10 minutes

Use
Always arrive on time.

Ingredients

◇ A large, dark glass bottle with a cork;
◇ Pocket watch;
◇ Full moon water;
◇ Four-leaf clover;
◇ Daffodil flowers;
◇ Golden glitter.
◇ Green candle for sealing.

Procedure

1. Insert the pocket watch into the bottle.
2. Add the four-leaf clover.
3. Add daffodil flowers.
4. Add a handful of gold glitter.
5. Fill with moon water.
6. Cork the bottle and place it on a protected surface (a saucer, a box, anything you don't mind ruining).
7. Light the green candle and wait for the wax to melt a little.
8. Being careful not to burn yourself, pour melted wax over the cap to seal your witch bottle.
9. Now your bottle is ready. Keep in mind that the auspicious day for fortune spells is Thursday, so if possible prefer Thursday to other days to consecrate your fortune bottle. Bury the bottle.

Witch Bottle To Always Find Parking

Difficuty
★ ★

Preparation Time
10 minutes

Use
finding parking on the first shot

Ingredients

- A large, dark glass bottle with a cork;
- Hypericum flowers;
- Four-leaf clover;
- Pen and paper;
- Selenite chips;
- Green candle for sealing.

Procedure

1. On a slip of paper write "There is always a free parking space for me wherever I am. This is how I want it and this is how it will be." Roll it up and put it in the bottle.
2. Enter the flowers of St. John's Wort.
3. Add selenite chips.
4. Add the four-leaf clover.
5. Cork the bottle and place it on a protected surface (a saucer, a box, anything you don't mind ruining).
6. Light the green candle and wait for the wax to melt a little.
7. Being careful not to burn yourself, pour melted wax over the cap to seal your witch bottle.
8. Now your bottle is ready. Keep in mind that the auspicious day for fortune spells is Thursday, so if possible prefer Thursday to other days to consecrate your fortune bottle. Bury the bottle.

Witch Bottle To Bestow Good Fortune On Someone

Difficuty

*

Preparation Time

10 minutes

Use

finding someone who can help you

Ingredients

- A large, dark glass bottle with a cork;
- Photo of the person;
- Acorn;
- Emerald;
- Three four-leaf clovers;
- Honey;
- Green candle for sealing.

Procedure

1. Take the photo of the person to whom you want to give good luck, roll it up and dip it in honey, then insert it into the bottle.
2. Insert acorn.
3. Add the emerald.
4. Add three four-leaf clovers.
5. Cork the bottle and place it on a protected surface (a saucer, a box, anything you don't mind ruining).
6. Light the green candle and wait for the wax to melt a little.
7. Being careful not to burn yourself, pour melted wax over the cap to seal your witch bottle.
8. Now your bottle is ready. Keep in mind that the auspicious day for luck spells is Thursday, so if possible prefer Thursday to other days to consecrate your bottle of luck. Bury the bottle near the chosen person's house, unbeknownst to him or her.

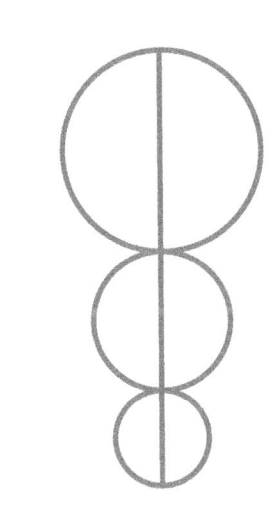

- CHAPTER 8 -

Jar Spell Recipes For Physical And Spiritual Healing

Witch Bottle To Propitiate Calmness

Difficuty
*

Preparation Time
10 minutes

Use
to propitiate calm and relaxation

Ingredients

◊ A medium-sized dark glass bottle with a cork;
◊ White rose petals;
◊ Amethyst chips;
◊ Pink Himalayan salt;
◊ Dried lavender sprig;
◊ Chamomile flowers;
◊ Dried sage leaves;
◊ Eggshells;
◊ Blue candle for sealing;

Procedure

1. Insert white rose petals into the bottle.
2. Insert the amethyst chips into the bottle, one at a time. There is no specific number to be met: when you feel it is enough, stop.
3. Insert dried sage leaves into the bottle.
4. Cover the whole with pink Himalayan salt.
5. Insert chopped (not crumbled or pulverized) egg shells into the bottle.
6. Stuff the lavender sprig and chamomile flowers into the bottle.
7. Cork the bottle and place it on a protected surface (a saucer, a box, anything you don't mind ruining).
8. Light the blue candle and wait for the wax to melt a little.
9. Being careful not to burn yourself, pour melted wax over the cap to seal your witch bottle.
10. Now your bottle is ready. Keep in mind that Thursday is auspicious for the consecration of physical and spiritual healing spells, so if possible prefer Thursday to other days to consecrate your healing bottle.
11. Keep your healing bottle under your pillow for three nights and three days (make sure the pillowcase is made of a natural material such as cotton or silk).

Witch Bottle To Ward Off Nightmares

Difficulty
★ ★

Preparation Time
10 minutes

Use
propitiate I am serene and without nightmares

Ingredients

◇ A medium-sized dark glass bottle with a cork;
◇ Dried lavender sprig;
◇ Dried chamomile flowers;
◇ Rose thorns;
◇ Homemade and totally natural rose water;
◇ Dried sage leaves;
◇ Amethyst chips;
◇ Yellow silk ribbon (or square of yellow silk or cotton);
◇ Yellow candle for sealing;

Procedure

1. Insert seven rose thorns into the bottle, one at a time.
2. Insert the yellow ribbon or square into the bottle.
3. Insert seven amethyst chips into the bottle, one at a time.
4. Insert dried sage leaves into the bottle.
5. Stuff the lavender sprig and chamomile flowers into the bottle.
6. Cork the bottle and place it on a protected surface (a saucer, a box, anything you don't mind ruining).
7. Light the blue candle and wait for the wax to melt a little.
8. Being careful not to burn yourself, pour melted wax over the cap to seal your witch bottle.
9. Now your bottle is ready. Keep in mind that Thursday is auspicious for the consecration of physical and spiritual healing spells, so if possible prefer Thursday to other days to consecrate your healing bottle.
10. Keep your healing bottle under your pillow for seven days and seven nights (make sure the pillowcase is made of a natural material such as cotton or silk).

Witch Bottle To Propitiate Creativity

Difficuty
*

Preparation Time
10 minutes

Use
to propitiate calm and relaxation

Ingredients

◇ A large dark glass bottle with a cork;
◇ Wood fern;
◇ A handful of dried rosemary;
◇ A handful of dried basil;
◇ Pine needles;
◇ Acacia honey;
◇ An object that has to do with creativity (example: a pen for writers, a brush or pencil for artists, and so on);
◇ Orange candle for sealing.

Procedure

1. Insert the wood fern into the bottle.
2. Insert a handful of dried rosemary into the bottle.
3. Place a handful of dried basil in the bottle.
4. Insert the pine needles into the bottle, one at a time.
5. Dip the object of creativity (pen, brush, etc.) in acacia honey until it is thoroughly saturated, then place it in the bottle.
6. Cork the bottle and place it on a protected surface (a saucer, a box, anything you don't mind ruining).
7. Light the orange candle and wait for the wax to melt a little.
8. Being careful not to burn yourself, pour melted wax over the cap to seal your witch bottle.
9. Now your bottle is ready. Keep in mind that Thursday is auspicious for the consecration of physical and spiritual healing spells, so if possible prefer Thursday to other days to consecrate your healing bottle.
10. Keep your bottle to propitiate creativity in the room where you usually practice your creative hobbies, or in your office. The important thing is that it is not visible or reachable by anyone.

Witch Bottle For Emotional Healing

Difficuty
*

Preparation Time
5 minutes

Use
healing emotional wounds

Ingredients

◇ A medium-sized dark glass bottle with a cork;
◇ Seven peppermint leaves;
◇ Ivy sprig;
◇ Cypress sprig;
◇ Black tourmaline chips;
◇ One garlic rib;
◇ Disinfectant;
◇ Gauze square;
◇ Blue candle for sealing.

Procedure

1. Insert the ivy sprig and the cypress sprig.
2. Insert the peeled garlic rib into the bottle.
3. Insert seven black tourmaline chips into the bottle, one at a time.
4. Insert the seven peppermint leaves into the bottle, one at a time.
5. Dip the gauze square in the disinfectant, wring out the excess then insert it into the bottle.
6. Cork the bottle and place it on a protected surface (a saucer, a box, anything you don't mind ruining).
7. Light the blue candle and wait for the wax to melt a little.
8. Being careful not to burn yourself, pour melted wax over the cap to seal your witch bottle.
9. Now your bottle is ready. Keep in mind that Thursday is auspicious for the consecration of physical and spiritual healing spells, so if possible prefer Thursday to other days to consecrate your healing bottle.
10. Keep your healing bottle under your pillow for seven days and seven nights (make sure the pillowcase is made of a natural material such as cotton or silk).

Witch's Bottle To Propitiate Forgiveness And Let It Flow

Difficuty
*

Preparation Time
10 minutes

Use
forgetting wrongs done and forgiving

Ingredients

◊ A medium-sized dark glass jar with a cork stopper-it is important that it has a wide opening to allow the ingredients to pass through;
◊ One white onion;
◊ Photo of the person to be forgiven;
◊ Pink silk ribbon;
◊ Pink candle for sealing.

Procedure

1. Cut the onion in half and insert the two halves into the jar, making sure that the cut side is facing the other (as if to close it);
2. Insert the photo of the person to be forgiven in between the two halves. If the photo is too large you can fold it in half.
3. Cork the jar and place it on a protected surface (a saucer, a box, anything you don't mind ruining).
4. Tie the pink ribbon on the neck of the jar, securing the cap. Make a triple knot.
5. Light the pink candle and wait for the wax to melt a little.
6. Being careful not to burn yourself, pour the melted wax over the cap to seal your witch bottle. It is not a problem if the wax gets on the ribbon.
7. Now your bottle is ready. Keep in mind that Thursday is auspicious for the consecration of physical and spiritual healing spells, so if possible prefer Thursday to other days to consecrate your healing bottle.
8. Keep your healing bottle under your bed until thinking about that person you no longer feel resentment or resentment, and you feel your heart light.

Witch Bottle For Healing From Childhood Trauma

Difficuty: ★★

Preparation Time: 10 minutes

Use: healing from childhood traumas and wounds

Ingredients

◇ A medium-sized dark glass bottle with a cork;
◇ Black rock salt;
◇ Rock crystal (hyaline quartz);
◇ Rose quartz chips;
◇ A small object from your childhood (if you don't have one, a picture of you as a child is fine).
◇ Pen and paper;
◇ Large lime tree leaf;
◇ Calendula oleolite;
◇ Green candle for sealing.

Procedure

1. Create a base in the bottle with black salt;
2. Insert the rock crystal into the bottle;
3. Insert the rose quartz chips into the bottle, one at a time. There is no exact amount, when it is enough you will feel it yourself.
4. Wrap your childhood object in the lime leaf, then insert it into the bottle.
5. Insert drops of oleolite reciting, "May this bottle heal my past wounds and protect me from future wounds intended for me."
6. Cork the bottle and place it on a protected surface (a saucer, a box, anything you don't mind ruining).
7. Light the green candle and wait for the wax to melt a little. In the meantime, take a few minutes to meditate on your childhood trauma.
8. Being careful not to burn yourself, pour the melted wax over the cap to seal your witch bottle. It is not a problem if the wax gets on the ribbon.
9. Now your healing bottle is ready. Keep in mind that Thursday is auspicious for the consecration of physical and spiritual healing spells, so if possible prefer Thursday to other days to consecrate your healing bottle.
10. Keep your healing bottle under your bed until you feel you have left your traumatic past behind once and for all.

THE JAR SPELLS

Witch's Bottle For Inner Peace

Difficuty ★ ★ ★

Preparation Time 15 minutes

Use achieving inner peace

Ingredients

◊ A small, dark glass bottle with a cork;
◊ Jasmine flowers;
◊ Sprig of chasteberry;
◊ Lapis lazuli chips;
◊ Sodalite chips;
◊ Moon eclipse water;
◊ Freshly picked moss;
◊ Eucalyptus essential oil;
◊ Blue candle for sealing.

Procedure

1. For a more intense effect, you can dress your candle with eucalyptus essential oil (movement from the center inward to help it obtain) and chamomile and calendula flowers;
2. Insert jasmine flowers;
3. Insert eight lapis lazuli chips into the bottle, one at a time.
4. Insert eight sodalite chips into the bottle, one at a time.
5. Insert the freshly picked moss into the bottle;
6. Stuff the sprig of chasteberry into the bottle;
7. Pour eight drops of eclipse moon water;
8. Pour in eight drops of eucalyptus essential oil;
9. Cork the bottle and place it on a protected surface (a saucer, a box, anything you don't mind ruining).
10. Light the blue candle and wait for the wax to melt a little.
11. Being careful not to burn yourself, pour melted wax over the cap to seal your witch bottle.
12. Now your bottle is ready. Keep in mind that Thursday is auspicious for the consecration of physical and spiritual healing spells, so if possible prefer Thursday to other days to consecrate your healing bottle.
13. Keep the bottle with you at all times, in a pocket or purse.

Witch Bottle To Promote Acceptance

Difficuty
★

Preparation Time
10 minutes

Use
acceptance

Ingredients

◇ A medium-sized dark glass bottle with a cork;
◇ Azurite;
◇ Amethyst chips;
◇ Dried rosemary sprig;
◇ Cinnamon stick;
◇ Orange blossom;
◇ Lavender Oleolite;
◇ Pink candle for sealing.

Procedure

1. Insert eight amethyst chips into the bottle, one at a time.
2. Insert the orange blossoms into the bottle;
3. Insert azurite into the bottle;
4. Stick the rosemary sprig and cinnamon stick into the bottle;
5. Pour in eight drops of lavender oleolite essential oil;
6. Cork the bottle and place it on a protected surface (a saucer, a box, anything you don't mind ruining).
7. Light the pink candle and wait for the wax to melt a little.
8. Being careful not to burn yourself, pour melted wax over the cap to seal your witch bottle.
9. Now your bottle is ready. Keep in mind that Thursday is auspicious for the consecration of physical and spiritual healing spells, so if possible prefer Thursday to other days to consecrate your healing bottle.
10. Keep the bottle under the pillow as long as you deem necessary.

Witch's Bottle For Lucid Dreams

Difficuty
★ ★

Preparation Time
10 minutes

Use
promoting lucid dreams

Ingredients

◇ A medium-sized dark glass bottle with a cork;
◇ Myrrh;
◇ Camphor essential oil;
◇ Chamomile flowers;
◇ Hypericum flowers;
◇ Fluorite chips;
◇ Biodegradable silver glitter;
◇ Rose water;
◇ Silver candle for sealing.

Procedure

1. Insert eight fluorite chips into the bottle, one at a time.
2. Place chamomile and St. John's Wort flowers in the bottle;
3. Pour in eight drops of camphor essential oil;
4. Slip a handful of myrrh into the bottle;
5. Pour in a spoonful of biodegradable glitter (make sure it's not plastic!).
6. Fill the bottle three-quarters full with rosewater;
7. Cork the bottle and place it on a protected surface (a saucer, a box, anything you don't mind ruining).
8. Light the silver candle and wait for the wax to melt a little.
9. Being careful not to burn yourself, pour melted wax over the cap to seal your witch bottle.
10. Now your bottle is ready. Keep in mind that Thursday is auspicious for the consecration of physical and spiritual healing spells, so if possible prefer Thursday to other days to consecrate your healing bottle.
11. Keep the bottle under your pillow. Before you go to sleep, take the bottle and shake it so that the glitter spreads into the water, then put it back under your pillow. Replace it when the glitter has completely dissolved.

Witch's Bottle For Astral Travel

Difficuty ★ ★ ★

Preparation Time 15 minutes

Use to encourage astral travel

Ingredients

◇ A medium-sized dark glass bottle with a cork;
◇ Belladonna berries (caution, it is toxic. Do not ingest and handle with proper precautions).
◇ Devil's claw;
◇ 8 bay leaves;
◇ Sea salt;
◇ Biodegradable silver glitter;
◇ Full moon water;
◇ Silver candle for sealing.

Procedure

1. Insert nightshade berries and bay leaf into the bottle;
2. Stuff a devil's claw flower into the bottle;
3. Place three tablespoons of sea salt in the bottle;
4. Pour in a spoonful of biodegradable glitter (make sure it's not plastic!).
5. Fill the bottle three-quarters full with full moon water;
6. Cork the bottle and place it on a protected surface (a saucer, a box, anything you don't mind ruining).
7. Light the silver candle and wait for the wax to melt a little.
8. Being careful not to burn yourself, pour melted wax over the cap to seal your witch bottle.
9. Now your bottle is ready. Keep in mind that Thursday is auspicious for consecrating physical and spiritual healing spells, so if possible prefer Thursday to other days to consecrate your healing bottle.
10. Keep the bottle under your pillow. Before you go to sleep, take the bottle and shake it so that the glitter spreads into the water, then put it back under your pillow. Replace it when the glitter has completely dissolved.

Witch's Bottle To Replenish Energy

Difficuty
*

Preparation Time
10 minutes

Use
recharging energetically

Ingredients

- A medium-sized dark glass bottle with a cork;
- Bay leaves;
- Agate;
- Sunshine water;
- Euphorbia;
- Lavender essential oil;
- Yellow candle for sealing.

Procedure

1. Insert the bay leaf into the bottle;
2. Insert euphorbia into the bottle.
3. Insert the agate into the bottle.
4. Fill the bottle three-quarters full with sun water.
5. Add a few drops of lavender essential oil.
6. Cork the bottle and place it on a protected surface (a saucer, a box, anything you don't mind ruining).
7. Light the yellow candle and wait for the wax to melt a little.
8. Being careful not to burn yourself, pour melted wax over the cap to seal your witch bottle.
9. Now your bottle is ready. Keep in mind that Thursday is auspicious for the consecration of physical and spiritual healing spells, so if possible prefer Thursday to other days to consecrate your healing bottle.
10. Keep the bottle under the pillow.

Witch Bottle To Purify From Negative Energies

Difficuty
★ ★

Preparation Time
10 minutes

Use
purify from negative energies

Ingredients

◊ A medium-sized dark glass bottle with a cork;
◊ Artemisia;
◊ Euphorbia;
◊ Acacia honey;
◊ Bamboo;
◊ Sapphire;
◊ Black candle for sealing

Procedure

1. Insert mugwort into the bottle.
2. Insert euphorbia and bamboo into the bottle.
3. Insert the sapphire into the bottle.
4. Add three tablespoons of acacia honey.
5. Add a handful of black salt.
6. Cork the bottle and place it on a protected surface (a saucer, a box, anything you don't mind ruining).
7. Light the black candle and wait for the wax to melt a little.
8. Being careful not to burn yourself, pour melted wax over the cap to seal your witch bottle.
9. Now your bottle is ready. Keep in mind that Thursday is auspicious for the consecration of physical and spiritual healing spells, so if possible prefer Thursday to other days to consecrate your healing bottle.
10. Whenever you feel the need to purify yourself squeeze the small bottle in your hands and meditate for ten minutes, then put it away in a place out of sight of others.

Bottle of Witch for Gratitude

Difficuty *

Preparation Time 10 minutes

Use to be grateful, to feel gratitude

Ingredients
- A medium-sized dark glass bottle with a cork;
- Peppermint;
- Ivy;
- Lime leaf;
- Black tourmaline chips;
- Yellow candle for sealing.

Procedure
1. Insert peppermint into the bottle.
2. Insert ivy and lime leaf into the bottle.
3. Insert black tourmaline chips into the.
4. Cork the bottle and place it on a protected surface (a saucer, a box, anything you don't mind ruining).
5. Light the yellow candle and wait for the wax to melt a little.
6. Being careful not to burn yourself, pour melted wax over the cap to seal your witch bottle.
7. Now your bottle is ready. Keep in mind that Thursday is auspicious for the consecration of physical and spiritual healing spells, so if possible prefer Thursday to other days to consecrate your healing bottle.
8. Whenever you feel the need to feel more gratitude squeeze the small bottle in your hands and meditate for ten minutes, then put it away in a place out of sight of others.

Witch's Bottle For Happiness

Difficuty
★

Preparation Time
10 minutes

Use
leaving behind sadness and melancholy

Ingredients

◇ A medium-sized dark glass bottle with a cork;
◇ Basil;
◇ Gattaria;
◇ Lime leaf;
◇ Sunflower seeds;
◇ Yellow candle for sealing.

Procedure

1. Insert the basil into the bottle;
2. Insert the catwoman into the bottle.
3. Add the linden leaf.
4. Pour in a handful of sunflower seeds.
5. Cork the bottle and place it on a protected surface (a saucer, a box, anything you don't mind ruining).
6. Light the yellow candle and wait for the wax to melt a little.
7. Being careful not to burn yourself, pour melted wax over the cap to seal your witch bottle.
8. Now your bottle is ready. Keep in mind that Thursday is auspicious for consecrating physical and spiritual healing spells, so if possible prefer Thursday to other days to consecrate your healing bottle.
9. Whenever you need to feel more happiness squeeze the small bottle in your hands and meditate for ten minutes, then put it away in a place out of sight of others.

Witch's Bottle To Overcome a Disappointment

Difficuty: ★

Preparation Time: 10 minutes

Use: overcoming a disappointment

Ingredients

◊ A medium-sized dark glass bottle with a cork;
◊ Sage;
◊ Citrine quartz;
◊ Olive sprig;
◊ Coarse salt;
◊ White candle for sealing.

Procedure

1. Fill the bottle halfway with rock salt.
2. Insert the sage into the bottle.
3. Add citrine quartz.
4. Add the olive sprig.
5. Cork the bottle and place it on a protected surface (a saucer, a box, anything you don't mind ruining).
6. Light the yellow candle and wait for the wax to melt a little.
7. Being careful not to burn yourself, pour melted wax over the cap to seal your witch bottle.
8. Now your bottle is ready. Keep in mind that Thursday is auspicious for consecrating physical and spiritual healing spells, so if possible prefer Thursday to other days to consecrate your healing bottle.
9. Keep the bottle under your pillow.

Witch Bottle for Family Serenity

Difficuty *Preparation Time* *Use*

★ 10 minutes serenity in the family

Ingredients

◊ Four medium-sized dark glass bottles with corks;
◊ Rose petals;
◊ Hyaline quartz;
◊ Sodalite chips;
◊ Cluster of white sage;
◊ Lavender essential oil;
◊ White candle for sealing.

Procedure

1. Insert rose petals.
2. Insert sodalite chips, one for each family member (including animals).
3. Add hyaline quartz.
4. Have the bunch of white sage burned at home, collect the ashes and pour a teaspoonful into the bottle.
5. Add three drops of lavender essential oil.
6. Repeat the process four times to get a total of four bottles.
7. Cork the bottles and place them on a protected surface (a saucer, a box, anything you don't mind ruining).
8. Light the white candle and wait for the wax to melt a little.
9. Being careful not to burn yourself, pour the melted wax over the caps of the bottles to seal them.
10. Now your bottles are ready. Keep in mind that Thursday is auspicious for consecrating physical and spiritual healing spells, so if possible prefer Thursday to other days to consecrate your healing bottle.
11. Hide bottles in the four cardinal points of the house.

Witch Bottle To Boost Self-Confidence

Difficuty
★ ★

Preparation Time
20 minutes

Use
having confidence in one's abilities

Ingredients

◇ A medium-sized dark glass bottle with a cork;
◇ Rosemary;
◇ Sandalwood;
◇ Ambrosia;
◇ Agate;
◇ Orange candle for sealing.

Procedure

1. Have the sandalwood burn, collect the ashes, and put them in the bottle once cooled.
2. Add rosemary.
3. Add ragweed.
4. Add agate.
5. Cork the bottles and place them on a protected surface (a saucer, a box, anything you don't mind ruining).
6. Light the orange candle and wait for the wax to melt a little.
7. Being careful not to burn yourself, pour the melted wax over the bottle cap to seal it.
8. Now your bottle is ready. Keep in mind that Thursday is auspicious for the consecration of physical and spiritual healing spells, so if possible prefer Thursday to other days to consecrate your healing bottle.
9. Whenever you need self-confidence, squeeze the small bottle in your hands and meditate for ten minutes, then put it away in a place out of the sight of others.

Witch's Bottle To Reach A Healthy Weight

Difficuty ★ ★

Preparation Time 20 minutes

Use to achieve a healthy weight

Ingredients

◊ A medium-sized dark glass bottle with a cork;
◊ A photo of your ideal fitness weight;
◊ Coffee grounds;
◊ Thyme sprig;
◊ Fossil wood;
◊ Yellow candle for sealing.

Procedure

1. Fill the bottle halfway with coffee grounds.
2. Take a picture of your ideal form weight, roll it up and bury it in coffee grounds.
3. Insert the thyme sprig.
4. Add fossil wood.
5. Cover everything with coffee grounds until full.
6. Light the yellow candle and wait for the wax to melt a little.
7. Being careful not to burn yourself, pour the melted wax over the bottle cap to seal it.
8. Now your bottle is ready. Remember that Thursday is auspicious for consecrating physical and spiritual healing spells, so if possible prefer Thursday to other days to consecrate your healing bottle.
9. Whenever you need self-confidence, squeeze the small bottle in your hands and meditate for ten minutes, then put it away in a place out of the sight of others.

Witch Bottle To Stop Thinking Too Much

Difficulty
*

Preparation Time
10 minutes

Use
stop brooding about the past, present or future.

Ingredients

- A medium-sized dark glass bottle with a cork;
- Lavender flowers;
- Violets;
- Amethyst chips;
- Lavender essential oil;
- Purple candle for sealing.

Procedure

1. Insert the amethyst chips into the bottle.
2. Add lavender flowers.
3. Add violets.
4. Pour in a few drops of lavender essential oil.
5. Cork the bottle and place it on a protected surface (a saucer, a box, anything you don't mind ruining).
6. Light the orange candle and wait for the wax to melt a little.
7. Being careful not to burn yourself, pour the melted wax over the bottle cap to seal it.
8. Now your bottle is ready. Remember that Thursday is auspicious for consecrating physical and spiritual healing spells, so if possible prefer Thursday to other days to consecrate your healing bottle.
9. Whenever you need to relax and stop thinking squeeze the small bottle in your hands and meditate for ten minutes, then put it away in a place out of sight of others.

Witch Bottle For The Here And Now

Difficuty

★

Preparation Time

10 minutes

Use

Reconnecting with the here and now

Ingredients

◊ A medium-sized dark glass bottle with a cork;
◊ Rose petals;
◊ Lavender flowers;
◊ Jasmine;
◊ Myrrh;
◊ Brown candle for sealing.

Procedure

1. Insert rose petals;
2. Insert lavender flowers;
3. Add jasmine;
4. I add myrrh.
5. Cork the bottle and place it on a protected surface (a saucer, a box, anything you don't mind ruining).
6. Light the brown candle and wait for the wax to melt a little.
7. Being careful not to burn yourself, pour the melted wax over the bottle cap to seal it.
8. Now your bottle is ready. Remember that Thursday is auspicious for consecrating physical and spiritual healing spells, so if possible prefer Thursday to other days to consecrate your healing bottle.
9. Whenever you need to relax and stop thinking squeeze the small bottle in your hands and meditate for ten minutes, then put it away in a place out of sight of others.

Conclusion
The Magic Begins With You

We have reached the end of this compendium, but your path to Witchcraft is only beginning. With constant practice you will improve daily, and in no time you will become a skilled witch capable of creating your own grimoire containing your own recipes and rituals.

As you learned while reading this compendium, witch bottles are an age-old tradition that, if mastered correctly, can help you achieve incredible results. But don't be discouraged if results are slow to come at first, because you will learn what works for you through practice. We are not all the same: what works for someone may be a failure for someone else. Every witch must have the chance to make mistakes; only then can she learn and improve herself.

Witchcraft is not just a practice, but a way of life, a conscious choice to pursue the path of magic to improve your own life and the lives of others. It is a path that begins from within yourself, from knowing yourself and your abilities. Only from deep familiarity with your power can the roots of a competence develop that will lead you to do great things.

The magic begins with you.

Made in the USA
Las Vegas, NV
13 October 2022